Alaska Airlines

─ A VISUAL CELEBRATION ─

CLIFF & NANCY HOLLENBECK

Alaska Airlines

Authors Cliff and Nancy Hollenbeck
Published by Hollenbeck Productions
www.hollenbeckproductions.com

FIRST EDITION ©2012

Library of Congress Control Number 2011930280
International Standard Book Number 9781578335374

Design by Nancy Hollenbeck
Graphics by idesign, llc (Seattle)
Aircraft illustrations ©Mike Tobin
Illustrations are not to scale

Printed in China by Everbest Printing Co Ltd
Representatives: Alaska Print Brokers
Anchorage, Alaska

(*cover*) *Alaska Airlines Collection: Clay Lacy Aviation: Chad Slattery Photo*
An Alaska Airlines Boeing 737-800 is airborne above the clouds.

(*title page*) An Alaska Airlines Boeing 737-200 taxis across the frozen tarmac at Deadhorse Airport, Prudhoe Bay, Alaska. It was photographed at high noon during the Arctic Winter, with an outside air temperature of -50° Fahrenheit.

(*shown on this page*) In the early morning dawn, an Alaska Airlines Boeing 737-400 rises from the small airport at the Red Dog zinc and lead mine near Kotzebue, Alaska. The mine contracts with the airline to fly workers to and from Anchorage.

(*back cover*) *Alaska State Library Juneau: Mary Nan Gamble Collection*
A McGee Stinson airplane, the founding aircraft of Alaska Airlines, was "trim" in contrast to the old mule team. Aviation has certainly changed since 1932.

TECK Alaska Collection: Larry Hanna Photo

An Alaska Airlines Boeing 737-800 flies above the towering peak of Washington State's Mount Rainier.

A window view from an Alaska Airlines 737-800 symbolically shows the shadow of an early Alaskan bush plane against the spectacular scenery of the airline's namesake state, representing the past and present of this great carrier.

INTRODUCTION

On a cold 1932 winter morning, where the temperature has been known to reach -80° Fahrenheit, and in the middle of a country-wide economic depression, a struggling and nearly broke businessman, Linious "Mac" McGee, did the almost unthinkable. He started a one-plane airline in the Territory of Alaska. The primary mission of his risky, new enterprise was to transport trappers and their furs between Bristol Bay and Anchorage. It was his second foray into Alaska's still adolescent world of flight and, as fate would have it, the launch of an extraordinary and continuing saga like no other in the history of aviation.

Through some eighty years of mergers, purchases and back-room deals, McGee Airways has grown into one of the most successful and admired airlines in the world. Alaska Airlines. Today this vibrant air carrier group operates a fleet of some 165 aircraft and serves 90 cities in Alaska, Hawaii, Canada, Mexico and across the continental United States, with a growing force of nearly 13,000 dedicated and professional employees.

This book is a visual celebration of Alaska Airlines, through its historical roots, aircraft, printed materials, memorabilia and people. Thankfully, as the age of aviation came into practical use, so did the camera, which has provided a wealth of incredible material. We've had the pleasure of sorting through family photo collections, museum libraries, forgotten newspaper articles, the extensive Alaska Airlines archives, historical books and our own files. We have chosen what we feel are the most descriptive and interesting images. Many of these photos have never been published before, and the older historical images have been carefully restored as close to their original condition as possible.

Current and retired employees, families and friends of the airline have contributed and helped us assemble this chronicle. Their names appear in the book's final pages. Everyone has done their best to ensure that dates, names, locations and descriptions are accurate. We wish some of the founders were still with us to consult. Considering that over 80 years have passed since the beginning, what we have been able to accomplish is remarkable.

Personally, this has been an ideal project for us. Among Nancy's first memories is a seven-hour DC-4 trip from Anchorage to Seattle, with her father at the controls. Her uncle worked in Nome for McGee, Lavery and Mirow. Captain Chuck Davis, Nancy's father, worked at Merrill Field and later flew for Art Woodley's PNA. Cliff's father took flight training with Shell Simmons in Yakima, Washington. After serving in Vietnam, Cliff worked for Bill Tobin at the *Anchorage Times*, illustrator Mike Tobin's father. We met and married while at Wien Consolidated Airlines in Anchorage. Because of Nancy's hijacking incident, we wrote manuals and lectured on air safety. Cliff was employed at Alaska Airlines, getting an inside look at the airline and making lifetime friendships, before leaving to freelance as a writer and photographer.

Alaska Airlines has supported our creative endeavors for decades, and several examples appear in these pages. For us, this book is the perfect way to say thank you. We hope our friends at Alaska Airlines ... past and present, whether executives, flight crews, mechanics or baggage handlers ... will feel a sense of pride when they look through this book. We also know that, while cameras have been able to record a fascinating and often colorful history, neither pictures nor words can fully communicate the adventuresome spirit and loyalty of the people who are Alaska Airlines today and yesterday. They are an amazing group of people, who continue to be the heart of an amazing airline.

Please accept our work in the spirit it was created ... with gratitude and joy. We are pleased and honored to have played a part in the visual history of Alaska Airlines and in authoring this book.

— *Cliff and Nancy Hollenbeck*

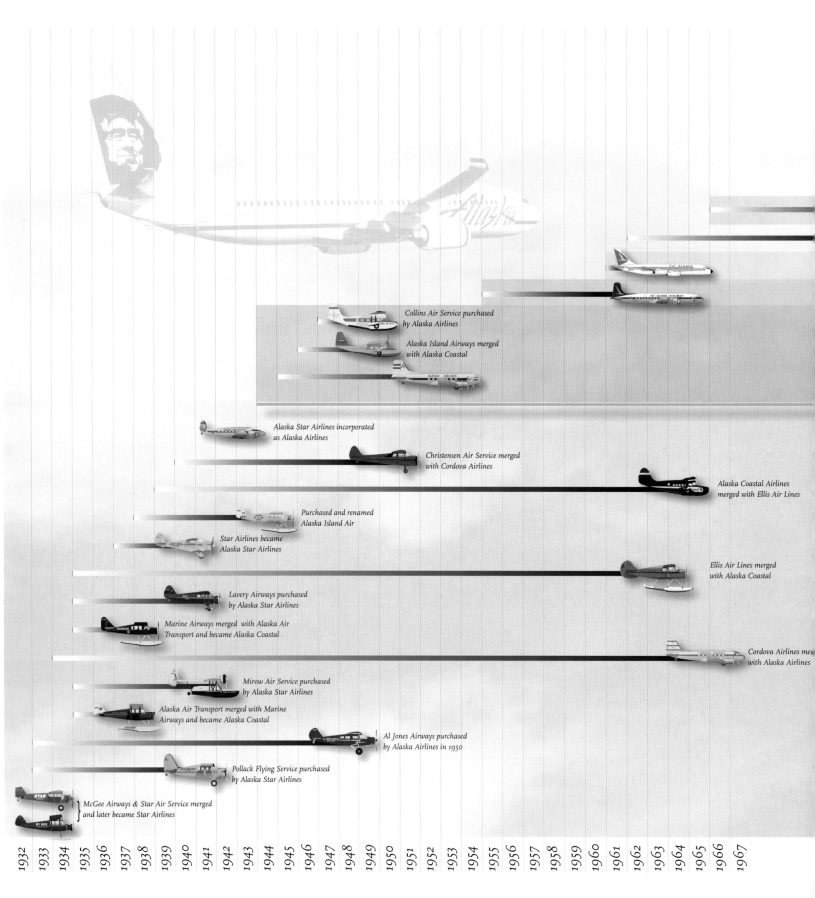

Modern Alaska Airlines | **1990-today**

Horizon Air | **1981-today**

Jet America | **1981-1987**

The Smiling Eskimo | **1976-1990**

The Spirit of Alaska | **1973-1976**

The Golden Samovar Era | **1969-1973**

The Golden Nugget Era | **1966-1972**

Alaska Coastal-Ellis | **1962 -1968**

The Jet Age | **1961-today**

The Golden Eagle Era | **1955-1966**

Collins Air Service | **1947-1950**

Alaska Island Airways | **1946-1951**

The Starliner Era | **1945-1955**

Alaska Airlines (inc.) | **May 2, 1944**

Alaska Star Airlines | **1942-1944**

Christensen Air Service | **1940-1952**

Alaska Coastal Airlines | **1939-1965**

Petersburg Air Service | **1938-1946**

Star Air Lines | **1937-1942**

Ellis Air Lines | **1936-1965**

Lavery Airways | **1936-1942**

Marine Airways | **1936-1939**

Cordova Airlines | **1934-1968**

Mirow Air Service | **1934-1942**

Alaska Air Transport | **1934-1939**

Al Jones Airways | **1933-1950**

Pollack Flying Service | **1933-1942**

Star Air Service | **1932-1934**

McGee Airways | **1932-1934**

*Collins Air Service purchased
by Alaska Airlines*

*Alaska Island Airways merged
with Alaska Coastal*

*Alaska Star Airlines incorporated
as Alaska Airlines*

*Christensen Air Service merged
with Cordova Airlines*

*Alaska Coastal Airlines
merged with Ellis Air Lines*

*Purchased and renamed
Alaska Island Air*

*Star Airlines became
Alaska Star Airlines*

*Ellis Air Lines merged
with Alaska Coastal*

*Lavery Airways purchased
by Alaska Star Airlines*

*Marine Airways merged with Alaska Air
Transport and became Alaska Coastal*

*Cordova Airlines me[rged]
with Alaska Airlines*

*Mirow Air Service purchased
by Alaska Star Airlines*

*Alaska Air Transport merged with Marine
Airways and became Alaska Coastal*

*Al Jones Airways purchased
by Alaska Airlines in 1950*

*Pollack Flying Service purchased
by Alaska Star Airlines*

*McGee Airways & Star Air Service merged
and later became Star Airlines*

1932 1933 1934 1935 1936 1937 1938 1939 1940 1941 1942 1943 1944 1945 1946 1947 1948 1949 1950 1951 1952 1953 1954 1955 1956 1957 1958 1959 1960 1961 1962 1963 1964 1965 1966 1967

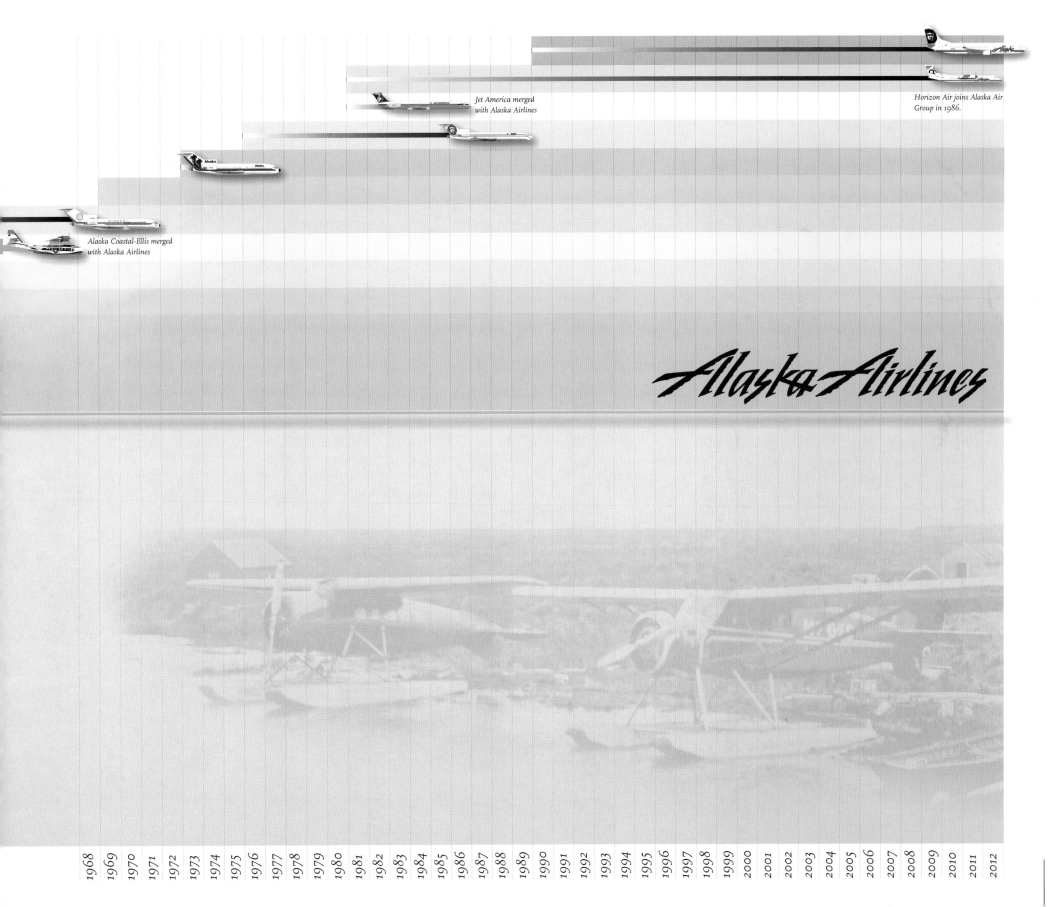

Alaska Coastal-Ellis merged
with Alaska Airlines

Jet America merged
with Alaska Airlines

Horizon Air joins Alaska Air
Group in 1986.

Alaska Airlines

1968 1969 1970 1971 1972 1973 1974 1975 1976 1977 1978 1979 1980 1981 1982 1983 1984 1985 1986 1987 1988 1989 1990 1991 1992 1993 1994 1995 1996 1997 1998 1999 2000 2001 2002 2003 2004 2005 2006 2007 2008 2009 2010 2011 2012

7

1932 - 1934

Late in the fall of 1929, as the stock market crashed and the Great Depression began, Linious "Mac" McGee stowed away aboard the *Aleutian*, a steamship bound from Seattle to Alaska. The 30-year-old Indiana native had been unsuccessful at homesteading in Montana and thought things would be better back in Alaska, where he had worked in the gold mines as a younger man.

McGee arrived in Anchorage with a $1.65 in his pocket, earned as a dishwasher, after a sympathetic steward gave him a job to pay for passage. McGee went right to work driving a Standard Oil Company truck and built a nest egg, which he invested to become a fur trader. It didn't take long to find that transporting furs by small boat and dog sled was too time consuming.

Teaming up with the legendary barnstorming bush pilot Harvey Barnhill, McGee bought a Stinson airplane to haul furs. The pair bought a second Stinson plane, but Barnhill & McGee Airways didn't last much longer. They dissolved the business, each taking an airplane.

A few days later, on a cold morning in 1932, Mac McGee launched McGee Airways. He was successful enough, in a short time, to buy back the other Stinson that Barnhill had kept. The mold had

been cast for an airline that eventually would grow into Alaska Airlines. In two short years of operating, McGee pioneered the concept of having a fleet of similar aircraft, so that parts and pilots would be interchangeable, and he established an aviation radio network.

McGee was more interested in business than he was in flying and he had a very strong work ethic. Despite his hard work and many innovations, he was on the brink of financial disaster most of the time. His pilots were often paid more than he was because of the sales commission system he devised. Plus, with a growing number of competitive new airlines in the territory, he was struggling to survive. In 1934, he sold McGee Airways and his seven silver-and-black Stinsons to Star Air Service for $50,000.

McGee ran Star Air Service for a brief time when his payments weren't made. He was asked to return a second time after one of the founders died in a crash, and McGee bought a majority share in the company. After an Alaskan mining family bought him out, he ran a successful liquor store and, later, a placer gold mine at Manley Hot Springs, near Fairbanks. He never returned to the airline business, but lived until 1988 and saw Alaska Airlines become a strong international carrier.

FLY AN HOUR OR WALK A WEEK

SERVING KANTISNA MINING Dist.

MᴄGEE AIRWAYS

(inset) Alaska Aviation Museum Anchorage

(photo) University of Alaska Fairbanks: Kay J. Kennedy Collection

(inset) This hand-painted sign advertised the benefit of flying McGee Airways in the early 1930s. Today it hangs in the Alaska Aviation Museum in Anchorage.

(photo) This McGee Airways Stinson SM-8A is one of the first aircraft owned by what is now Alaska Airlines. The three-seat single-engine floatplane was bought by Linious "Mac" McGee in 1932 and initially flew between Anchorage and Bristol Bay, Territory of Alaska. After changing pontoons, the airplane is being transported along an Anchorage street.

(*inset*) Linious "Mac" McGee stands by one of his Stinson SM-8As on skis. A fur parka and mukluks protect him from the icy winter weather in Bristol Bay.

(*back*) Three black and silver Stinson SM-8As, with skis in place of their pontoon floats, show McGee's economical decision to fly a fleet of similar aircraft so that parts could be interchangeable and pilots would all be trained on the same equipment.

(*inset*) Linious "Mac" McGee, founder of McGee Airways, stands between A.C. "Chet" McLean (left) part owner of the airline, who flew as a pilot for Ketchikan Airways and Panhandle Air Transport Company; and Johnny Amundsen, another noted commercial pilot of the 1930s in Alaska. They were meeting at Boeing Field in Seattle, Washington, outside the Washington Air Services office.

(*back*) A beautiful single-engine McGee Airways Stinson Reliant SR-5 prepares for takeoff from the ice-covered waters on Anchorage Bay.

(*inset*) *Don "Bucky" Dawson Collection; Lloyd R. Jarman Photo*
(*back*) *Alaska Aviation Museum Anchorage*

(*inset*) A McGee Airways mechanic works on a Stinson aircraft in the airline's Anchorage hangar.

(*back*) A McGee Airways Stinson SM-8A floatplane sits on the muddy tide-flats of Cook Inlet alongside Emard Cannery near Anchorage. The picture was taken in the summer of 1937 or 1938.

(top) Museum of Flight Seattle: Robert W. Stevens Collection
(bottom left & right) Virgil Hanson Family Collection

McGee Airways radio operator Virgil Hanson and his wife, Josephine "Lila" (Hugh), in 1937 on Third and I streets in Anchorage. Hanson was the first full-time radio operator for the airline.

Virgil Hanson at work in the Anchorage office. He began his career with McGee Airways, continued with Star Air Lines and retired from Alaska Airlines.

(top) A McGee Airways Stinson SM-8A floatplane rests along the shore of the Chena River in Fairbanks, in 1935.

STAR AIR SERVICE
FLIGHT ★ INSTRUCTION
ANCHORAGE ALASKA

1932 - 1934

Not long after McGee Airways began hauling furs from the bush, a group of flight instructors and businessmen in Seattle saw the growing need for pilots in Alaska and founded Star Air Service Flight Instruction in 1932. While Star had a thriving business training pilots down south, its chief pilot and partner, Stephen "Steve" Mills, thought it would be more profitable to offer that service in Anchorage. He also reasoned it would be better to train pilots under the same conditions in which they would be flying.

Along with his partners, Iowa pharmacist Jack Waterworth and a former student, Canadian Charles Ruttan, who had loaned them money to replace their first crashed airplane, the group borrowed enough money from a wealthy Alaskan miner to ship a small Fleet Biplane to Seward and then fly it to Merrill Field, Anchorage.

After a strong beginning, business slowed and they began offering charters. It still wasn't enough to pay all the bills so Ruttan joined the Anchorage Fire Department and Waterworth worked part time in a local drug store. Business increased, but Star was temporarily shut down again after a pilot crashed their only plane. The partners again took day jobs and worked on their plane at night.

Another investor loaned them money to buy a Curtiss Robin and they became a successful two-plane airline. Business continued to improve and their fleet of aircraft grew, along with the competition. It was difficult to make enough money to survive the winter slowdowns. Star's owners approached Linious McGee to talk about a merger and were surprised when he offered to sell his airline and seven aircraft. He set a price and offered to carry a contract, with the stipulation that he would run the airline if their payments were slow. They agreed, and the purchase created the largest airline in Alaska with 22 aircraft.

McGee wasn't being paid a year later, so he returned to manage the airline until receiving all of his money. Shortly after McGee left, Steve Mills perished in a crash. So McGee returned once again to run the airline and buy Waterworth's share. He expanded the business by buying struggling Alaska Interior Airlines, a carrier founded by one of McGee's first pilots, Oscar Winchell.

Ruttan left Star in the late 1930s when he purchased an oil distributorship. In late 1937, increasingly frustrated by the growing presence of federal regulators in Alaska skies, McGee sold the airline to a group of investors led by another of his former pilots and a successful mining family in Kuskokwim, Alaska (near Bethel). The new owners changed the name from Star Air Service to Star Air Lines. It would eventually become Alaska Star Airlines, along with Mirow Air Service, Lavery Air Service and Pollack Flying Service. In 1942, Alaska Star would change its name again to Alaska Airlines. McGee Airways and Star Air Service would forever be the colorful foundation of this great airline.

STAR AIR
SERVICE
★ FLIGHT ★
INSTRUCTION
ANCHORAGE ALASKA

(inset) Alaska Aviation Museum Anchorage
(photo) University of Alaska Fairbanks: Kay J. Kennedy Collection

(*inset*) A hand-painted wooden sign advertising Star Air Service flying lessons in 1930s Anchorage.
At the time, Anchorage was a town of just over 2,000 people in the Territory of Alaska.

(*photo*) A Star Air Service Bellanca Skyrocket floatplane is tied along a shoreline in central Alaska in 1937.

(*top*) Star Air Service founder, Stephen "Steve" Mills, in his winter fur parka and hat.

(*bottom*) Steve Mills in front of "North Star," a Fleet B-5 flight training biplane, the airline's first aircraft. Pilot Jack Waterworth is in the cockpit, getting ready for takeoff at Merrill Field in Anchorage.

(*top*) *Museum of Flight Seattle: Robert W. Stevens Collection*
(*bottom*) *Alaska Aviation Museum Anchorage: Babs Peck Photo*

(*top left*) A Star Air Service Bellanca Pacemaker beside a gravel runway in Anchorage.

(*top right*) A pilot delivers the mail from the pontoon float of a Star Air Service Bellanca Pacemaker. Natives used seal-skinned kayaks to retrieve arriving packages.

(*bottom*) The Star Air Service ticket office on Fourth Street in Anchorage, next to Hewitt's Photo Shop, in the early 1930s.

(top left) Alaska Aviation Museum Anchorage
(middle) Museum of Flight Seattle: Robert W. Stevens Collection
(bottom) Alaska Airlines Collection

(top left) Star Air Service mechanics work on a Bellanca Skyrocket floatplane in 1934 Anchorage.

(middle) With a Bellanca Pacemaker behind them, the principals of Star Air Service pose for their 1934 New Year's holiday card. From the left: pilot Aaron J. Valley; mechanic Elmer Nelson; William Earl Dunkle, Star financer and gold miner; Charles Ruttan, Star partner, office manager and pilot; CAA Inspector Hugh Brewster; mechanic Burris Smith; Charlie Bissel, mechanic, carpenter and fabric man; and Stephen "Steve" Mills, airline founder, president and pilot.

(bottom) A hand-colored photo of a Star Air Service Bellanca Pacemaker on skis sits along a snow-covered runway against the backdrop of mountains glowing in the sunshine. Snowshoes lean against the aircraft.

(next page) Irene Irvine, next to a Fleet B-5 biplane, was one of Star Air Service's first student pilots. Star initially planned to concentrate on flight training and occasionally handle charters.

POLLACK FLYING SERVICE

1933 - 1942

Pioneer bush pilot Frank Pollack began his flying career in the early 1930s in Valdez, Alaska, where he provided flight instruction to future Governor William A. Egan. Along with partner Edward Lerdahl, Pollack flew a small Lambert-powered Monocoupe and a single-seat Bush Pup.

Business was good enough to help Pollack move to Fairbanks in 1933, where he formed a larger flight instruction business and then established Pollack Flying Service. Along with his wife, Hazel, he took a daring contract with the U.S. Weather Bureau to fly weather instruments at an altitude of 18,000 feet without the aid of oxygen or a radio. A natural teacher, he was instrumental in helping younger pilots attain their ratings during his years in Fairbanks. Several students went on to fly with Northern Consolidated Airlines and Pan American Airways.

Pollack Flying Service was one of the more successful early airlines in the Territory of Alaska because of their monopoly serving mining and fishing camps out of Fairbanks and their charters throughout Interior Alaska. They also employed several excellent mechanics and were known to buy, repair and sell broken down planes from other small airlines.

As a result of this continuing success, Pollack Flying Service's routes and aircraft became an attractive potential addition to larger carriers. Pollack was purchased by Alaska Star Airlines in 1942, where its founder continued to work for a time as operations manager in Fairbanks. This acquisition was just two years before Alaska Star Airlines incorporated as Alaska Airlines.

A female passenger's legs appear in the doorway of this Pollack Flying Service Bellanca Senior Pacemaker airplane on a Seattle airport tarmac.

POLLACK FLYING SERVICE

01175

POLLACK FLYING SERVICE
Fairbanks

(*inset*) Ticket stub for a Fairbanks flight on Pollack Flying Service, issued in the early 1930s.

(*back*) A Fairchild American Pilgrim sits outside the Pollack Flying Service hangar in Fairbanks.

22

The Pollack Flying Service hangar in Fairbanks. From the left: Robert W. "Bob" Ausley, Terry McDonald, Clyde Smith, Ernest Hubbard, Ray Pratt, Herm Joslyn, Ray Robinson and Jim Hutchison, with the company's 1930s Chevrolet truck and Stinson Reliant SR-9.

(*top*) Pollack Flying Service ground personnel ready sled dogs to board their Bellanca Senior Pacemaker along an icy runway.

(*bottom*) The young founder and president of Pollack Flying Service, Frank Pollack, in his winter fur parka.

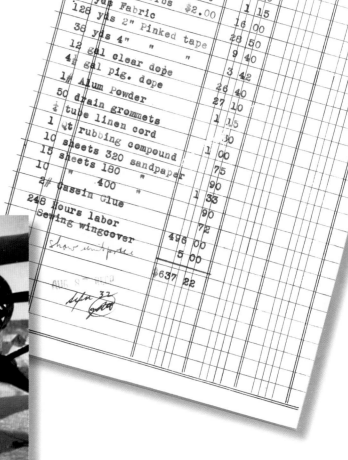

POLLACK FLYING SERVICE
FAIRBANKS, ALASKA. Aug 1 194_

M. Civil Aeronautics Administration
Anchorage, Als.

Repair of Bellanca Aircraft NC-799 W damaged
by C&A Aircraft NC-5

DATE	Material	CHARGES	CREDITS	BALANCE
	Cap Strip 1x1-60"	3 60		
	Spar Material			
	12 Ft Mah. Ply	6 00		
	Balsa 2X3X 58"	3 80		
1qt.	Varnish ½ Gal	1 70		
	Dope Proof Paint	2 10		
8	Bellanca ribs $2.00	1 15		
38 yds	Fabric	16 00		
128 yds	2" Pinked tape	28 50		
38 yds	4" "	9 40		
12 gal	clear dope	3 42		
4½ gal	pig. dope	26 40		
1#	Alum Powder	27 10		
50	drain grommets	1 15		
¼	tube linen cord	30		
1 qt	rubbing compound	1 00		
10	sheets 320 sandpaper	75		
15	sheets 180 "	90		
10	400 "	1 33		
2#	Casein Glue	90		
248	Hours labor	496 00		
	Sewing wingcover	72		
	show work flashed	5 00		
		$637 22		

(top) Pollack Flying Service in Fairbanks, from the left: Mechanic "Happy" Applegate, Lloyd Lounsbury, founder and President Frank Pollack, and Paul Lein.

(bottom) Lindy Brennan and Hazel Pollack, in fur parkas, alongside a Pollack Flying Service aircraft on an icy Fairbanks day.

(invoice) A Pollack Flying Service invoice for repair costs on their Bellanca aircraft damaged by a Civil Aeronautics Administration plane in 1941.

AL JONES AIRWAYS
BETHEL, ALASKA
1933 - 1950

A country boy from Knoxville, Tennessee, Al Jones, christened Algernon Sidney Jonez, (later changed to Jones) grew up to become one of Interior Alaska's most successful bush airline operators. Al Jones Airways may have finished strong, but it was a long and interesting path getting there.

The Jonez family moved to Seattle when Al was still a youngster, where he lived until serving in World War I. He became interested in aviation and flying during his military training, but didn't obtain a pilot's license. After the war, Jones followed his brothers to Alaska and worked for the Alaska Railroad Hospital in Anchorage. He married R. Lee Bartholf, a registered nurse and daughter of a well-known gold mining family, and they became the owners of the first airplane in Anchorage. Al Jones still didn't have a pilot's license and a pilot friend soon crashed the plane.

The couple moved to Hope, where Jones started a logging business, making wooden ties for the Alaska Railroad. They also ran a mink farm, were game guides for hunters and, in 1929, operated Kustatan Packing Company, a salmon cannery on Cook Inlet.

In 1933, the Joneses moved back to Anchorage. Al Jones was still interested in flying and finally got his pilot's license, bought his own aircraft, and began carrying passengers and freight commercially. This was the beginning of Al Jones Airways.

During World War II, Jones flew MATS (Military Air Transport Service) to Adak in the Aleutian Islands for the U.S. Army Air Force. After the war ended, Jones moved to Bethel and began operating his airline full time. Al Jones Airways grew rapidly and added more airplanes, including Jones' pride and joy, a Douglas DC-3 "Tundra Clipper." Unfortunately, just months after purchasing the DC-3, Jones crashed and perished in a Travelaire 6000 plane. He was on a mercy flight transporting frozen reindeer meat for Eskimo patients at Bethel Hospital. He lost his life on his 47th birthday, August 20, 1947. That wrecked Travelaire has been beautifully restored and now hangs in the Alaska Aviation Museum in Anchorage.

After Jones died, his second wife, Anne, took over operations of the airline until 1950, when Alaska Airlines purchased Al Jones Airways. Anne Jones continued working, doing public relations for a time at Alaska Airlines in Anchorage.

The Aviation Museum in Anchorage, Alaska, commissioned this beautiful painting by Evelyn Jones Peters, "Flying Home," to commemorate the museum's restoration of an Al Jones Airways Travelaire 6000B. Peters is a retired Coast Guard commander and noted artist, as well as the daughter of Al Jones.

(*top*) "This 1943 photo shows my father's devil-may-care attitude, with the look in his eye and the quirk to his mouth, as if he was going to tell a joke, which he did well," daughter, Evelyn Jones Peters, wrote.

(*bottom*) Pilot and airline President Al Jones with his Travelaire 6000B on an icy field in Bethel. A dog team and sled were used to transport cargo to and from the small aircraft.

(*next page*) Al Jones bought this beautiful Douglas DC-3 after World War II, just months before he was killed in a plane crash. The aircraft, which sits alongside a snow-covered runway at Merrill Field in Anchorage, served in the Alaska Airlines fleet until 1958.

AL JONES
AIRWAYS
1946
MERRIL FIELD

ALASKA AIR TRANSPORT

1934 - 1939

Adventure was the middle name of Sheldon Simmons. At 16, he quit school to become a deckhand aboard a freighter bound for the Orient. He later drove a delivery truck in Ketchikan, studied electrical engineering in Los Angeles and worked as an electrician in the Alaska-Juneau Mine. He quit the mine and sailed 2,100 miles down the Yukon River with a friend in a rowboat. When they landed in the Arctic, Simmons took a job on a runway construction project and got the flying bug watching bush planes land on the new airstrip.

Simmons returned to his boyhood home in Yakima, Washington, in 1929 to take flying lessons. With his new pilot's license, he went back to work at the mine in Juneau and also began restoring planes and honing his flying skills. He went to work for a small airline, but his plane was damaged in a storm and the owners couldn't afford to rebuild it. They sold the wreck for $1 to Simmons, who found investors to finance the rebuild and, with it, Alaska Air Transport was born. This was 1934 and Shell Simmons was only 26 years old. The rebuilt Stinson floatplane was put into service just as Pan American Airways closed its seaplane operations in Southeast Alaska. That left Simmons as the only operation in the area.

Simmons worked tirelessly at Alaska Air Transport, dropping mail and Christmas turkeys to miners and once hauling the Juneau marshal to a gun fight. He was the first commercial pilot to fly year-round in Southeast Alaska. When cash flow was tight, he'd accept company stock from his backers in lieu of a salary, eventually obtaining a majority holding. He was a skilled businessman who helped build a one-plane fleet into a major regional carrier, adding Bellancas and a Fairchild 71 to his fleet. He was an innovator constantly improving seaplane designs and engine performance, and he played a key role in gaining approval for instrument landings in Sitka and night flights at Juneau. His daring exploits often made headlines, but Shell Simmons was a good pilot and a entrepreneur at heart.

In 1939, he merged Alaska Air Transport with Alex Holden's Marine Airways to create Alaska Coastal Airlines. By then, Simmons was only 31. In 1962, Alaska Coastal merged with Ketchikan-based Ellis Air Lines to form the largest scheduled airline exclusively operating amphibian aircraft. They merged with Alaska Airlines in 1968, bringing Simmons and partner Bob Ellis to the Alaska Airlines Board of Directors, where Simmons served for 13 years.

An Alaska Air Transport Lockheed Vega floatplane sits in front of the airline's hangar on Gastineau Channel in 1930s Juneau.

This page

This page

(*top left*) Shell Simmons, Alaska Air Transport founder and president, is smartly dressed in a pilot's leather jacket, jodhpurs and high-laced boots in 1935.

(*top right*) Simmons stands on the float of his Aeromarine-Klemm plane by a Southeast Alaska tidewater glacier.

(*bottom*) An Alaska Air Transport Stinson SM-2 floatplane rests on a Southeast beach in the Territory of Alaska.

Page 32

These four treasured hand-tinted photographs hung on the wall of Shell Simmons' Juneau home.

(*top left*) His Lockheed Vega sits along a snow-covered shore and near a dog team in Southeast Alaska.

(*top right*) With the Alaska-Gastineau Mill and Gold Mine in the background, Simmons flies his highly modified Curtiss Jenny floatplane along the south Juneau shoreline.

(*bottom left*) Simmons flies a passenger along the Gastineau Channel, near Juneau, aboard his Aeromarine-Klemm floatplane.

(*bottom right*) Simmons used his Stinson floatplane to deliver mail into remote locations in Southeast Alaska.

(*top photos*) *Alaska Airlines Collection*
(*bottom*) *Alaska State Library Juneau: Shell Simmons Collection*

MIROW
AIR SERVICE

1934 - 1942

German immigrant Hans Mirow was working as an oiler on a merchant ship when he jumped ship in New York in 1933. His ambition was to become a commercial pilot, so he headed to the Territory of Alaska looking for a job. He was successful and flew with Northern Air Transport. A year later, he moved to Nome and started his own airline, Mirow Air Service.

Over the years, Mirow owned and flew no less than a dozen or so different types of aircraft, including a state-of-the-art 225 horse-powered Stinson SR-5 Reliant, which had the unusual luxury of a heated cabin. That aircraft is on display at the Alaska Aviation Museum in Anchorage. Mirow ran scheduled flights out of Nome, and often flew charters to the most remote parts of Alaska. The Air Service also frequently flew to Seattle, which became a huge part of the business.

Mirow was best known for making dozens of mercy flights in bad weather. He once rescued sailors from an ice-bound ship in the Arctic Ocean. Unfortunately, he crashed and died during one of those rescue flights in 1938, just outside the village of Kaltag on the Yukon River.

Mirow's widow, Madeline, operated the airline for a few years after his death. She hired Johnny Moore, a local bush pilot to help her with flights and the business, a partnership that led to marriage. When Star Airlines offered to buy Mirow Air Service in the spring of 1942, Madeline Mirow took the offer. Hans Mirow's airline, and his spirit of community service, lives on in today's Alaska Airlines.

A dog team rests in front of a Mirow Air Service Lockheed Vega in Alaska's Interior. The engine is draped with fire-resistant material that forms a duct around the aircraft's engine and directs heat from a gas burner to keep it from freezing. This photo was taken by Hans Mirow with one of the first Kodak box film cameras.

(*top*) Hans Mirow (*left*), founder of Mirow Air Service, helps work on his Stinson aircraft with pilot Ron Taylor and mechanic Warren Tillman.

(*bottom*) Sitting next to the Alaska Airmotive Company repair facility in Nome, a Mirow Sikorsky 539B draws curious onlookers.

(*top*) *Museum of Flight Seattle: Robert W. Stevens Collection*
(*bottom*) *Alaska Aviation Museum Anchorage*

(*top*) Martha Opland, dressed in a fur winter parka, next to a Mirow Air Service Stinson on the airfield in Nome. Her husband, Alfred Opland, regularly flew to points along the Bering Sea as part of the Federal Reindeer Acquisition Unit.

(*bottom*) Passengers deplane and cargo is unloaded from a Stinson Tri-Motor on skis at a snow-covered airstrip in Interior Alaska.

(*top*) Lars Opland Collection

(*bottom*) *Museum of Flight Seattle: Robert W. Stevens Collection*

Mail is unloaded from a Mirow Air Service Lockheed Vega on skis into a 1935 Nash.

(top) One of the Stinson Tri-Motors, chartered by the Reindeer Acquisition Unit in the 1930s, sits along a gravel runway in springtime Nome.

(bottom) Mirow Air Service workers take a break at the airfield in Nome. A Lockheed Vega sits on skis in the compact snow that is both a roadway for the company truck and a runway for its mail service.

(top) Lars Opland Collection
(bottom) University of Alaska Fairbanks Historical Collection

1934 - 1968

Cordova Air Service began in 1934 like other small airlines in Southeast Alaska. Modestly. It was formed by miners and businessmen who wanted air service out of their city, and operated by Kansas native M.D. "Kirk" Kirkpatrick, its only pilot for a time. Cordova was busy, if not financially successful, so Kirkpatrick hired fellow Kansas native and a friend-of-a-friend, Merle Smith, to help with the flying. Smith began his flying as a barnstormer and performed in a flying circus at county fairs in Kansas, Oklahoma and Nebraska. He hitchhiked to Seattle and rode a steamship to Cordova to start the new job.

Smith became a legend in Alaskan aviation, as much for his nickname as for his business success. Flying to the Bremner Mine early his first summer, Smith landed on a soggy tundra field. When attempting to take off after a heavy rain squall, a wheel on the aircraft dropped into a hole and the plane was flung around and nose-dived deep into the mud. Smith reported the incident to his boss over the radio, and a fellow bush pilot who heard the report christened him "Mudhole." The name stuck.

In 1939, Kirk Kirkpatrick was killed attempting to land in a snowstorm, and Mudhole Smith was asked to assume the presidency. He went to work making it one of the most successful airlines in Alaskan history, changing the name to Cordova Airlines in 1956,

In the mid 1960s, with several bush aircraft and DC-3s, C-46s and Convair 240s, Cordova Airlines was flying from its home base in Cordova to Yakutat, Juneau, Cape Yakataga, Chitina, McCarthy, Chisana and a northern leg to Dawson City in the Yukon Territory. Eventually the airline would also fly to Anchorage, Middleton Island, Homer, Kenai and Seldovia.

Cordova Airlines enjoyed an extensive route system, financial strength and owned the Anchorage-to-Juneau route that Alaska Airlines President Charlie Willis wanted when the two carriers merged in 1968. Alaska also acquired several experienced employees in the deal. Merle "Mudhole" Smith served on Alaska Airlines' Board of Directors until his death in 1981.

Merle "Mudhole" Smith was the perfect portrait of a dashing, young bush pilot in 1937. Leaning against the Cordova Air Service (later Cordova Airlines) open-cockpit Stearman biplane, Smith would go from pilot to president of the airline in 1939. Today this aircraft is at the Alaska Aviation Museum in Anchorage.

Alaska Airlines Collection

(top) A Cordova Air Service Bellanca CH-300 Pacemaker moored on Eyak Lake near Cordova during the summer of 1938.

(bottom) A Cordova Air Service Travelaire 6000A on skis parked next to the company hangar in Cordova.

(ad) Adding to its charm, a Cordova Air Service 1944 newspaper advertisement contains a few misspelled words.

(next page) Cordova Airlines President Merle "Mudhole" Smith stands beside the shining metal body of "St. Elias," a Lockheed Electra 10-B, while its wings beautifully reflect the snow in Anchorage. The aircraft was sold to Reeve Aleutian Airways in 1947.

CORDOVA AIRLINES
Flights Daily
SEWARD • VALDEZ • CORDOVA
Also Charter Trips

(top) A Cordova Airlines DC-3 sits on a snowy tarmac at Anchorage International Airport in 1957.

(bottom) Cordova Airlines pilot Albert Kulis and a flight attendant pose beside the company sign at the new Anchorage International Airport in 1953. A year later, as a first lieutenant in the Air National Guard, Kulis was lost at sea flying a P-80 over Goose Bay. Today Kulis Air National Guard base is named after him.

(wings) Captain Stanley Baumwald Collection
A dramatic set of Cordova Airlines pilot's hat wings.

(top & bottom) Robert W. Stevens Family Collection: Jim Connelley photo

(top) Two shining Cordova Airlines Douglas DC-3s sit near the runway at Anchorage International Airport in the 1960s. One of the most famous aircraft ever built, the dependable DC-3s are still in use today.

(bottom) A pilot looks through the slushy rainfall from the cockpit window of a Cordova Airlines DC-3.

(wings) Captain Stanley Baumwald Collection Cordova Airlines first officer's wing.

MARINE AIRWAYS
JUNEAU ALASKA

1936 - 1939

Veteran Southeast Alaska pilot, Canadian Alex Holden, never really thought about owning or running an airline. He loved flying, having learned with the RCAF (Royal Canadian Air Force) during World War I, and was content working for two or three successful airlines in the Territory of Alaska. He was at his happiest flying tourists to see glaciers in an open-cockpit Zenith biplane.

Holden did, however, say "yes" when Juneau charter boat operator and businessman James Davis walked into the Gastineau Hotel and asked a group of pilots if any of them wanted to start an airline. Davis carried mail and passengers to several small cities on his 64-foot boat, the *Estebeth*, but was losing business to the faster and more popular airlines, especially to Shell Simmons at Alaska Air Transport. He saw Holden as a key to getting a share in the new form of transportation business.

Together they formed Marine Airways during the summer of 1936. Their first airplane was an old Bellanca Pacemaker, nicknamed "Shaky Jake" by pilots and passengers alike. Holden became famous when writer Ernie Pyle, of the *Washington Daily*

News, flew with him and wrote: "I have complete confidence in a pilot who is bald-headed. And practically none at all in one with a mustache."

During its short life, Marine Airways was successful primarily because of a government contract to deliver once-a-week mail from its base in Juneau to Sitka, Chichagof and the other western islands. Marine made additional money by stopping along the way to pick up passengers at mining operations in Alaska and Canada.

For three years, Marine Airways competed with Alaska Air Transport until it was clear there was not enough business to support two independent airlines. Alex Holden merged his airline with competitor Shell Simmons in 1939, and they became Alaska Coastal Airlines. Together they co-managed the airline until Holden's death in 1952. In 1965, Simmons would merge Alaska Coastal with Ellis Air Lines to become Alaska Coastal-Ellis Airlines. Three years later, the carrier merged with Alaska Airlines.

(top left) Bodding Family Collection: Keith Petrich Photo
(top right) Alaska Aviation Museum Anchorage
(bottom) Bodding Family Collection

(top left) Marine Airways Bellanca Pacemaker taxies along the waterfront of downtown Juneau.

(top right) The Marine Airways hangar along the Juneau shoreline. Marine's Bellanca Pacemaker had wheels attached to its pontoon floats for easy maneuvering in and out of the water.

(bottom) Marine Airways Bellanca Pacemaker tied to the shoreline on Lake Union, Seattle, in 1937.

Lavery
AIRWAYS
1936 - 1942

The son of "Robert Lavery, a noble pioneer from New York," according to the *Fairbanks News Miner* daily newspaper, William "Bill" Lavery was born and spent most of his life in Fairbanks, Alaska. As a youngster, he worked in his father's general merchandise store, earning enough money to take flying lessons. It's said that he learned to fly long before learning to drive a car. He loved aviation and soon became an excellent airplane mechanic as well as a pilot.

Young William formed Lavery Airways in 1936, at the age of 20, establishing the first scheduled service between Fairbanks and Anchorage. Along with his wife, Sylvia, he ran the airline for a number of years, adding several aircraft and charter routes throughout the northern part of the state. Lavery was a good businessman, but he enjoyed getting out of the office and was the airline's busiest pilot.

William Lavery received the Order of Lenin in 1934 for rescuing Russian settlers after Chukchi Sea ice crushed their steamship *Cheliuskin* and left them stranded. Along with other pilots, Lavery landed on the frozen sea to help those who had survived. With the money awarded him for heroism by the Soviet government, he bought the first movie camera in Fairbanks and made films of life throughout Interior Alaska.

Lavery Air Service was successful, and its Fairbanks-to-Anchorage scheduled route was the perfect addition to Alaska Star Airlines. The much larger Alaska Star purchased Lavery in 1942, just two years before changing its name and incorporating as Alaska Airlines.

The young founder of Lavery Airways, William "Bill" Lavery, stands proudly beside his Stinson SR-5 Reliant in Nome.

Alaska Aviation Museum Anchorage

Alaska Aviation Museum Anchorage

(*top*) A Lavery Airways Stinson SR-5 Reliant and a Stinson Tri-Motor, parked at Merrill Field in Anchorage.

(*bottom*) A mechanic stands beside a Lavery Airways Aeronca.

(*top*) A late 1930s newspaper advertisement for Lavery Airways featured their modern eight-passenger Stinson Tri-Motor and fares between Fairbanks and Anchorage.

(*bottom*) Alaska Airmotive mechanics and Lavery pilots taking a smoke break beside Lavery Airways Stinson Reliants and an Aeronca in Nome.

1936 - 1965

Bob Ellis, a native of St. Albans, Vermont, entered the Naval Academy at age 16. Unfortunately, he left two years later when he learned that only a few of his class would receive commissions due to military spending cuts following World War I. A friend and fellow cadet, who grew up in Seattle, invited Ellis to the Northwest. He moved to Seattle and took a job as the chief and only pilot at Bryn Mawr airfield, today the Renton City Airport.

Ellis' stay was cut short when he learned about the first nonstop flight between Seattle and Juneau. Ellis talked his way onto that 1929 flight, serving as navigator. It was a record-breaking journey onboard a Lockheed Vega plywood floatplane, which took seven hours and thirty-five minutes en route. The crew was given a hero's welcome in Juneau and went on a barnstorming tour of Southeast Alaska. The charming New Englander had become an Alaskan for life.

He flew all over the state for a variety of airlines, landing on everything from ice fields to river bars. With a four-seat, single-engine Cabin Waco floatplane, he founded Ellis Air Transport in Ketchikan in 1936. Ellis incorporated his airline in 1940, calling it Ellis Air Lines. He may have been an airline president, but he was a bush pilot who loved serving his passengers. Customers and friends were scattered throughout Southeast communities.

When the Navy called during World War II, Ellis proudly served as a squadron and Kodiak Air Station commander. His wife, Peg, and two trusted employees kept the business going. After the war, he happily returned to provide flight service throughout Southeast Alaska. He increased his fleet with war-surplus planes, eventually totaling ten Grumman Goose amphibious aircraft. In addition to running the airline, Ellis served in the Territorial Senate, from 1955 to 1958, and was mayor of Ketchikan for a time.

Increasing government red tape, unions, geographical limits on expansion and heavy competition all lead to Ellis's decision to merge his airline with Juneau-based Alaska Coastal Airlines in 1965. Together they became Alaska Coastal-Ellis. Both were well-run airlines, had good equipment and personnel, and together they were even stronger. They were in a good position when larger airlines became interested in merging. Alaska Coastal-Ellis chose Alaska Airlines over Wien Consolidated because of Alaska's route to Seattle, merging in 1968. Bob Ellis served with distinction on the Alaska Airlines Board of Directors for 13 years. He never left his beloved home in Ketchikan, where he died in 1994 at the age of 91.

(top) A young Bob Ellis in the 1930s.

(bottom) Bob Ellis on the pontoon float of his Waco biplane in front of the Ellis Air Transport hangar in Ketchikan.

(patch) *Barry Washington Collection*
Ellis Air Lines embroidered pilot's patch.

ELLIS AIR LINES

ELLIS
AIR
LINES

Passengers	**Ellis Air Lines**	Air Express
Craig	Waterfall	Wrangell
Klawack	Rose Inlet	Petersburg
Hydaburg	All Canneries	Juneau
Belle Island	All logging camps	Fishing Trips

All points in southeastern Alaska

Connecting lines to
Sitka · Whitehorse · Seward · Haines · Fairbanks · Kodiak
Skagway · Anchorage · Nome
Via Pan American·Juneau
to Seattle

Charter planes for
6·5·4·3 & 1 passengers
Rates on Request

Phone 488

Office and waiting
room at 1277
Tongass Avenue

(top) Mary Goodwin Collection
(bottom) Don "Bucky" Dawson Collection
(next page) Bodding Family Collection: Lloyd Varman Photo

(top) The Ellis Air Lines hangars along the shoreline in Ketchikan. An Ellis Grumman Goose (left) is next to their Bellanca Pacemaker on floats.

(bottom) A 1946 Ellis Air Lines hand-painted sign hung in their booking office at the Ingersoll Hotel in downtown Ketchikan.

(life-ring) Ketchikan Museums

A life-ring used by Ellis Air Lines' amphibious fleet of Grumman Goose planes.

(next page) Gerald A. "Bud" Bodding takes off across Ketchikan's Tongass Narrows in an Ellis Air Lines Waco YKS-6.

TARIFFS *and* SCHEDULES

ELLIS AIR LINES — PASSENGER FARES

	WRANGELL	SITKA	PR. RUPERT	PETERSBURG	KLAWOCK	KETCHIKAN	JUNEAU	HYDABURG	EDNA BAY	CRAIG	ANNETTE
ANNETTE	41.40	72.00	41.40	46.80	37.80	10.80	72.00	37.80	46.80	37.80	—
CRAIG	51.84	48.60	51.84	56.70	1.80	27.00	79.38	9.00	27.00	—	21.00
EDNA BAY	59.94	45.00	59.94	64.80	27.00	36.00	87.48	36.00	—	15.00	26.00
HYDABURG	51.84	50.40	51.84	56.70	10.80	27.00	79.38	—	20.00	5.00	21.00
JUNEAU	39.60	—	82.62	36.00	79.38	61.20	—	44.10	48.60	44.10	40.00
KETCHIKAN	30.60	61.20	30.60	36.00	27.00	—	34.00	15.00	20.00	15.00	6.00
KLAWOCK	51.84	48.60	51.84	56.70	—	15.00	44.10	6.00	15.00	1.00	21.00
PETERSBURG	18.00	—	59.94	—	31.50	20.00	20.00	31.50	36.00	31.50	26.00
PR. RUPERT	55.08	82.62	—	33.30	28.80	17.00	45.90	28.80	33.30	28.80	23.00
SITKA	—	—	45.90	—	27.00	34.00	—	28.00	25.00	27.00	40.00
WRANGELL	—	—	30.60	10.00	28.80	17.00	22.00	28.80	33.30	28.80	23.00

Plus Federal Tax if Applicable   One-Way Fares in Lightface Type   Round-Trip Fares in Boldface Type

ELLIS AIR LINES

TARIFFS SCHEDULES

GOING YOUR WAY IN SCENIC SOUTHEASTERN ALASKA

fly with ELLIS AIR LINES

P. O. BOX 1059 • KETCHIKAN, ALASKA

(*schedule*) An early brochure of Ellis Air Lines fares and schedules.

(*bag*) An Ellis Air Lines flight bag, featuring the "peas and carrots" color scheme of their early aircraft.

fly with ELLIS AIR LINES

KETCHIKAN, ALASKA

(*brochure*) An early Ellis Air Lines tourism brochure for Southeast Alaska.

(*photo*) Ellis agent Jo Collins talks with pilot Leon Snodderly beside an Ellis Air Lines Grumman Goose at Annette Island, Territory of Alaska. The Ellis Goose shuttled passengers from the island to Ketchikan. Annette served as Ketchikan's connection to non-amphibious aircraft up until 1973, when the city's land airport opened on nearby Gravina Island.

(*pass*) Ellis Air Lines used a hand-painted Gate Pass in Ketchikan in 1955.

(*brochure*) Ellis Air Lines brochure explains how its amphibious aircraft took passengers from runways on Annette Island to water landings in Ketchikan.

(gate pass) Ketchikan Museums: Ed Baker Collection
(brochure) Barry Washington Collection

KETCHIKAN, ALASKA

WHAT... NO LANDING FIELD?

If you're bound for Ketchikan, Alaska, by air — you're flying to a city that has no landing field! But don't worry. You're in no danger of being tossed off your plane with a parachute and a prayer.

No . . . all Ketchikan passengers are landed in the usual manner at Annette Island, 21 miles from Ketchikan which is on another island, Revillagigedo (just say Revilla). Your ticket to Ketchikan carries a portion showing Annette to Ketchikan. That's the portion that entitles you to the 12-minute flight by an air carrier, unique — Ellis Air Lines.

You're now in Alaska. Ellis Air Lines will make every effort to get you to Ketchikan as soon as possible. If you've never flown in an amphibian, you'll find it's an interesting experience. As soon as your baggage can be transferred to the dependable, twenty-four passenger PBY you will be whisked to Ketchikan—and on the way there is marvelous scenery to enjoy. During the busy, tourist season it often takes several planes to speed you to Ketchikan and sometimes the planes must make two trips to accommodate everyone. But everyone gets to Ketchikan as promptly as Ellis can fly them there. It's really much like taking a limousine from, let us say, Los Angeles airport to downtown—and involves considerably less inconvenience. And where else have you been where the "limmo" flies?

While you're on Annette Island, you'd probably like to know something about it. It was given to the Tsimshian (Simp-shee-ann) Indians in 1887 by President Grover Cleveland. The Tsimshians paddled their great, open canoes to Annette from Old Metlakatla in British Columbia, led by an Episcopal missionary, Father Duncan. This man of vision and faith is still revered and his remembrance is kept fresh to this day by the Duncan Memorial Church in the village the Indians built. They called the village "New Metlakatla" and here they lived, sole proprietors of Annette Island. That was in 1887.

The years passed quietly in the little village until 1939, when the Civil Aeronautics Administration took steps to establish an air field at Annette, which is one of the very few flat places on the outside route along the southeast coast. Permission to build a base and air field at the southern end of the island was granted by the Metlakatlans.

21 MILES—ANNETTE ISLAND TO KETCHIKAN

METLAKATLA

DUNCAN MEMORIAL CHURCH

ANNETTE ISLAND

ANNETTE ISLAND AIRPORT

ELLIS AIR LINES

fly with **ELLIS** KETCHIKAN, ALASKA
AIR LINES

PAY ROLL

DATE	CHECK NO.	PAY TO THE ORDER OF			AMOUNT
SEP 30 59	12316	K.C. PERRY		2.36 $	2.36

ELLIS AIR LINES

MINERS AND MERCHANTS BANK
OF KETCHIKAN
KETCHIKAN, ALASKA   59-3

(*paycheck*) A $2.36 paycheck, issued to pilot K.C. Perry and signed by Ellis Air Lines' President Bob Ellis in 1959.

(*photo*) An Ellis Air Lines Consolidated PBY "Catalina" at the dock in Ketchikan.

STAR AIR LINES INC.

1937 - 1942

To understand Star Air Lines, you have to start from the beginning. Following the sale of McGee Airways to Star Air Service, and the fatal crash of Star's chief pilot and founder Steve Mills, Linious "Mac" McGee returned to the company. He managed the airline for a year, but became increasingly distressed by the growing presence of federal regulators in Alaska from the newly formed Civil Aeronautics Board (CAB). That new board would soon end the free-wheeling era of bush flying.

In late 1937, only five years after Star Air Service was formed, McGee sold the financially struggling airline to a group of investors led by one of his former pilots, Don Goodman, and a successful Kuskokwim mining family, David Strandberg and his sons. The new owners changed the name of the carrier, incorporating it as Star Air Lines. They operated a fleet of 15 different types of aircraft. Goodman established uniform passenger routes, rates and freight tariffs, and put pilots on salary instead of sales commissions to eliminate competition between the men.

Star Air Lines was the largest airline in Alaska in 1940. Following the CAB Alaska Aviation Hearings, Star received most of what it had requested, but still wanted a route between Alaska and Seattle. Alaska aviation had very little political strength in Washington, D.C., and when the CAB did award them the Seattle route in March 1941, Pan American Airways was successful in getting President Roosevelt to veto the new route.

Money was short, so in 1942 Star and Woodley Airways went to the CAB proposing a merger. The resulting airline would be called Alaska Airlines, but the merger was not approved. Woodley had the money to buy Star and asked a broker, Homer Robinson, to make the purchase. Unbeknownst to Woodley, Homer worked for Raymond Willett Marshall, a multimillionaire junk dealer from New York. Homer negotiated the sale of Star Air Lines, instead buying it for Marshall. On July 6, 1942, Star changed its name to Alaska Star Airlines. Art Woodley applied for the name Alaska Airlines, but his attorney failed to pay the $15 fee. Alaska Star quickly filed for the name, paid the fee and in May of 1944 was incorporated as Alaska Airlines.

NC10365

STAR AIR LINES INC

A Star Air Lines Bellanca Skyrocket is tied to a small dock at a remote lake near Anchorage.

When You Visit Alaska
Fly With
Star Air Lines

Anchorage, Alaska

(brochure & bottom photo) Alaska Aviation Museum Anchorage
(top photo) Eddie Coates Collection

(*brochure*) An early 1940s brochure showcases a Star Air Lines Fairchild Pilgrim on a wet landing field. This aircraft carried all cargo or could be converted to fly nine passengers.

(*top photo*) This Star Air Lines Bellanca CH-300 Pacemaker has balloon tires to give it traction through the snow and mud. Noted pilot Jack Jefford, in the fur parka and lace-up boots, stands at the right.

(*bottom photo*) A Star Air Lines Lockheed Orion 9 carried six passengers and showcased the airline's distinctive logo.

To Our
Alaskan Airplane Traveling Public

Star Air Lines, Inc.
ANCHORAGE, ALASKA

(*brochure*) Star Air Lines featured their four-place Beech F17D Staggerwing in this 1930s brochure. Owned by Star, the plane was used by the U.S. Air Force in 1942 and returned to airline service in 1949.

(*logo*) The Star Air Lines logo, featuring the black and international orange colors painted on their aircraft.

(*bottom*) A 1940s-vintage woody wagon parked beside a Star Air Lines Ford Tri-Motor at Merrill Field in Anchorage.

(all images) Ron Suttell Collection

PETERSBURG U.S. AIR MAIL SERVICE
1938 - 1946

Hollywood stunt pilot George S. "Tony" Schwamm and his wife, Kathryn, started their one-airplane Petersburg Air Service in the spring of 1938. Tony had starred as one of the pilots in the Howard Hughes movie *Hell's Angels* before leaving the film business to move to Petersburg, Alaska. In less than a year, he met registered nurse Kathryn Sims, fell in love, got married and started Petersburg Air Service.

Alaska State Library Historical Collection Juneau: Tony and Kathryn Schwamm beside their Waco in the late 1930s.

The small airline, flying a Curtiss Robin, specialized in roundtrips between Petersburg and Juneau, with Tony being the pilot and mechanic, and Kathryn the office manager and first woman radio operator in Southeast Alaska.

As business grew they were able to buy additional aircraft, first a Cabin Waco and then a Taylorcraft. The airline suspended operations during World War II while Tony Schwamm was on active duty as a lieutenant commander in the Navy Reserve. After the war, the airline started again with a Fairchild 24 and a TravelAire 6000.

When investors offered to buy the airline in 1946, the couple sold Petersburg Air Service and it was renamed Alaska Island Air. The Schwamms moved to Anchorage, where Tony Schwamm became the first director of aviation for the Territory of Alaska. He also became the manager of Anchorage International Airport, and was the Anchorage postmaster in 1963. He died of natural causes in Anchorage in 1966. Kathryn Schwamm lived to 101, passing away in California in 2005.

Mike Tobin Collection: A Petersburg Air Service Curtiss Robin docked in Juneau, Territory of Alaska, in the 1940s.

Christensen
AIR SERVICE
ALASKA

1940 - 1952

Hakon "Chris" Christensen, affectionately known as the "Flying Dane," was born in Denmark in 1902. He learned to fly in 1917 in his hometown of Pastbro, Denmark. After immigrating to America, Christensen worked as a barnstormer pilot in the Midwest, where he gained most of his early experience flying stunts and racing.

Christensen came to Alaska in 1933, after selling his plane to a man in Fairbanks and flying it up from Iowa for him. The following year, he became a pilot for the Cantwell Mining Company, flying a Curtiss Robin on freelance charters from Cantwell to Peters Creek Mine, Valdez Creek Mine, Anchorage and Fairbanks.

Christensen moved his small business to Anchorage in 1940 and formed Christensen Air Service. He established a passenger

COYOTES SHOT FROM PLANE
Anchorage, Alaska

Museum of Flight Seattle: Hewitt's Photo
Hakon Christensen beside one of his Waco aircraft on skis in the 1940s.

route between Anchorage and Seward. The route was so successful that Merle "Mudhole" Smith, president of Cordova Airlines and a long-time friend and fellow barnstormer, offered to buy the smaller company. Christensen sold his airline to Cordova in 1952.

While flying his Grumman Super Widgeon amphibious airplane from Seattle, Christensen and passenger, businessman and politician Wells Ervin, were hit by a severe storm between Yakutat and Cordova. Rescue planes were sent from the 10th Rescue Unit at Elmendorf Air Force Base, but Christensen perished in the crash. His passenger died later in a hospital. This was 1956, just four years after selling Christensen Air Service. He was gone before seeing his airline become part of the Alaska Airlines family.

1939 - 1965

Two small and successful airlines, Alaska Air Transport (AAT) and Marine Airways, joined forces to create Alaska Coastal Airlines in 1939. Shell Simmons of AAT and Alex Holden of Marine were both well-known pilots and businessmen in Southeast Alaska. The competition of the era had become intense and the new partners were right in thinking that a larger operation would be more successful. Once the Civil Aeronautics Authority approved the merger, Alaska Coastal Airlines had little competition in Southeast Alaska, except for Bob Ellis with his smaller Ellis Air Lines in Ketchikan.

Alaska Coastal Airlines managed its way through World War II and afterward began purchasing and flying surplus Navy PBY amphibious airplanes. Simmons had an engineering background and figured out how to improve the aircraft's instrumentation so his pilots could land at night in Juneau and make instrument approaches to Sitka. They extended their schedule, flying up to 16 hours a day. Simmons was the first commercial pilot to fly year-round in Southeast Alaska.

Coastal's innovative maintenance staff converted the old Navy patrol bombers into passenger-ready planes, and invented new tools and procedures to deal with issues such as constant saltwater corrosion and often-freezing winter weather. The staff solved the challenge of getting planes into their hangar during low tides, which could vary by some 20 feet, by using an old hotel elevator motor, Caterpillar cylinder and a sturdy cable system to create a crane lift.

Alaska Coastal grew and prospered, operating for 26 years. A good share of the credit belonged to the airline's manager and bookkeeper, O.F. "Ben" Benecke, who co-managed with Shell Simmons. Benecke was a tireless worker, who joined the company right before World War II.

On April Fool's Day of 1962, Alaska Coastal Airlines merged with Ellis Air Lines, and the combined carrier began operating as Alaska Coastal-Ellis Airlines. Their new carrier was in business six years and then merged into Alaska Airlines in 1968. Shell Simmons and Bob Ellis joined Alaska's Board of Directors, as did their manager, Ben Benecke, who also served as Alaska Airlines president from 1973 to mid-1976.

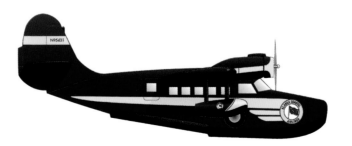

(*top*) An Alaska Coastal Airlines Consolidated PBY Catalina is parked on a Southeast Alaska airport ramp between flights.

(*tool*) *Barry Washington Collection*. Alaska Coastal Airlines pilots used a handmade metal Load Adjuster to calculate weight and balance.

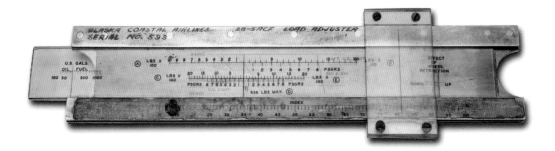

William Stedman Collection

(*above*) An Alaska Coastal Airlines Bellanca Pacemaker, known as "Shaky Jake," after landing passengers next to the towering ice face of Mendenhall Glacier, near Juneau.

(*next page top*) An Alaska Coastal Airlines Lockheed Vega on floats at the downtown Juneau "Seadrome" hangar.

(*next page bottom*) Two amphibious Grumman Goose aircraft, flown by Alaska Coastal Airlines and Ellis Air Lines, are tied dockside in the waters off Ketchikan. Both airlines operated a fleet of these sturdy aircraft, which became legendary in opening Southeast Alaska Territory to commercial aviation.

(*next page brochure*) A 1950s Alaska Coastal Airlines brochure invites visitors to explore Southeast Alaska.

(top) Ron Suttell Collection
(bottom) Ketchikan Museums
(brochure) Jeff Cacy Collection

N47M

ALASKA COASTAL AIRLINES

ACA
ALASKA Coastal AIRLINES

invites you to

Explore

Scenic Southeastern

Alaska

ALASKA COASTAL AIRLINES

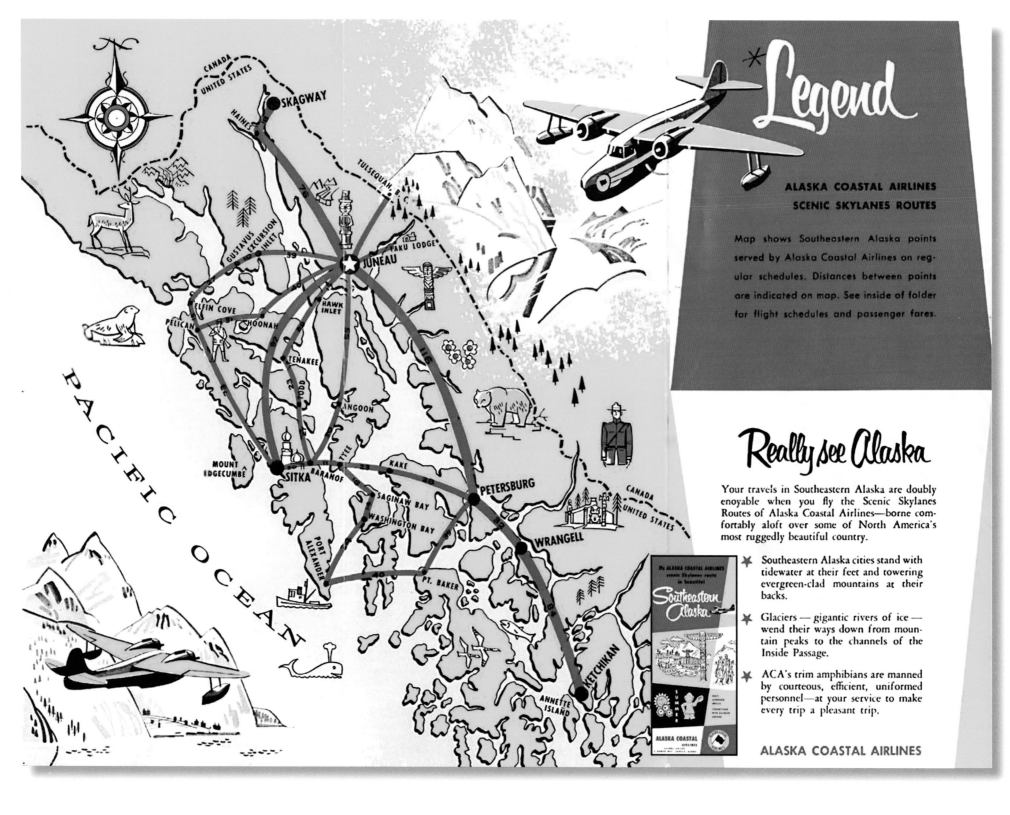

Alaska State Library Juneau: Shell Simmons Collection

(*above*) A hand-colored photo of an Alaska Coastal Airlines Consolidated PBY Catalina moves through the cold waters and small islands near Sitka, with Mount Edgecumbe in the background.

(*wings*) *Captain Stan Baumwald Collection*. A beautiful set of Alaska Coastal Airlines pilot's wings. They were U.S. Air Force wings with the Coastal logo attached.

(*previous page*) A colorful Alaska Coastal Airlines route map showing the extent of Southeast Alaska destinations serviced by their amphibious fleet.

(*above*) The thriving Alaska Coastal Airlines operation kept the shoreline along Juneau busy with Grumman Goose aircraft coming and going.
Winches hauled the huge amphibious aircraft from the water for servicing and repairs in Alaska Coastal's large hangars.

(*next page*) An Alaska Coastal Airlines Convair 240 flies above Alaska's snow-covered mountains and glaciers.

1942 - 1944

Alaska Star Airlines was never really founded. The carrier was mostly a name and logo change made in 1942 by the new owner of Star Air Lines, Raymond W. Marshall, a multimillionaire junk dealer from New York.

Marshall kept Star Air Lines at arm's length, often dumping his salvaged parts on the airline to make a profit without regard for the company. He frequently changed management and expanded the route system by buying smaller carriers: Lavery Airways, Mirow Air Service and Pollack Flying Service. According to reports, the manager of a separate Marshall company would buy a smaller airline and then resell it to Star Air Lines for double the amount in stock to Marshall. As a result, Marshall soon owned more than 80 percent of the company. With the mergers taking effect, the board at Marshall's direction made the name change on July 6, 1942, to Alaska Star Airlines. Its name lasted a short life span, but gave Alaska Airlines the ASA designation it has today.

The coming of World War II saw many ASA pilots leave for military service, but also brought in a lot of business servicing the new military airfields and supply depots. The airline grew despite the shortage of help, continuing feuds with the new Civil Aeronautics Board and cash shortages due to the distant owner's tightfisted methods.

The airline bought its first multi-engine aircraft, a Lockheed Lodestar, using an investment from Texas wildcatter Theodore "Ted" Law. Because of his investment, Law was soon named president of Alaska Star Airlines. The carrier operated for about two years before filing for one last name change on September 16, 1943. Attorneys for Woodley Airways had filed with the state for the "Alaska Airlines" name, but forgot to pay the $15 filing fee. Marshall's own attorney was nearby and quickly filed on behalf of Alaska Star Airlines, making sure to pay the fee. Less than a year later, in 1944, the company incorporated as Alaska Airlines.

An Alaska Star Airlines Lockheed Lodestar, purchased in 1943, flies past the towering wind-swept peak of Mount McKinley.

ALASKA STAR AIRLINES

(*photo*) An Alaska Star Airlines Bellanca sits on the dirt ramp
outside the airline's hangar at Merrill Field in Anchorage.

(*wings*) *Captain Stan Baumwald Collection*
Alaska Star Airlines pilot's wings.

(map & photo) Alaska Airlines Collection

(above) Alaska Star Airlines mechanics break from working on a Bellanca aircraft. From left: Roy Lefler, Tony Johansen, Oscar "Swede" Jensen and Charles Bisell.

(map) Alaska Star Airlines had an extensive route system within the Territory of Alaska in the early 1940s, stretching from Juneau in Southeast almost to Siberia at Gambell Island to Kotzebue above the Arctic Circle and across to Whitehorse in the Canadian Yukon Territory.

ALASKA STAR AIRLINES

Watch Alaska!

AT no time in the history of the Territory of Alaska has there been so much bristling activity as in the past eighteen months. Today, a vital stronghold in our all-out war effort . . . tomorrow, a land of untold opportunity for aggressive post-war development.

Keeping pace with present day air traffic requirements and gearing up for the passenger, mail, express and freight transportation needs of the morrow, ALASKA STAR AIRLINES has vastly increased its facilities—adding eight airplanes to its fleet; two new ground radio communication stations; a new, completely equipped, major overhaul station at Anchorage.

ALASKA STAR AIRLINES, having recently acquired the operation and equipment of Mirow Air Service, has extended the Nome-Anchorage run 600 miles southeastward to Juneau. A new passenger, mail route has been established between Fairbanks and Kodiak, with daily service to Anchorage, and scheduled service inaugurated between Nome and Fairbanks.

Today, ALASKA STAR activities are confined largely to essential military requirements, providing the most comprehensive transportation facilities available in the Alaskan Territory. At this time, ASA's fleet of 24 radio equipped transports maintains scheduled runs between 21 key cities, from which points 53 additional important destinations are quickly accessible via frequent ALASKA STAR operated non-schedule connecting flights. ASA is building today for a brighter tomorrow. *Watch Alaska—grow!*

It seems only yesterday that dog teams took days to cover territory Alaska Star planes now fly in a few hours.

For schedules, rates and other information consult The Official Aviation Guide

ALASKA STAR
AIRLINES

SERVING THE TOP OF THE WORLD

NOVEMBER 1942

(*above*) An illustrated 1940s brochure depicts the dashing Lockheed Lodestar zooming by the mountains of Alaska. At the time, this aircraft was the fastest twin-engine airliner in the world, cruising at more than 210 mph.

(*right*) In November of 1942, Alaska Star Airlines ran this advertisement to promote its World War II support efforts and declare its enthusiasm for development of the Territory of Alaska.

On its delivery flight to Alaska in 1943, this Lockheed 18 Lodestar was the first modern multi-engine airliner in the territory. Named "Starliner Anchorage," it was put into service between Juneau, Anchorage and Fairbanks.

May 2, 1944

Alaska Airlines was incorporated in the Territory of Alaska on May 2, 1944. Raymond W. Marshall's board of directors had voted to change the name from Alaska Star Airlines to Alaska Airlines a year earlier on July 6, 1943. However, it took that year and a lucky bit of legal maneuvering to even get ownership of the name. Woodley Airways had first laid claim to the name, filing for it in Juneau, but forgetting to pay the $15 filing fee. Alaska Star Airlines did a quick filing, with the fee, to acquire the name.

Texas oilman and Alaska Star Airlines investor and president, Theodore "Ted" Law, continued in office, becoming the first president of newly minted Alaska Airlines. He would leave the airline business in less than a year, clashing with Marshall's business style. Most of Law's investment was used to purchase aircraft and money was still short, so they initially resorted to

painting over the "Star" on aircraft, hangars and ticket offices, leaving a lopsided Alaska Airlines logo. At the time of incorporation, a new era of aviation was also coming to the Territory of Alaska. World War II was ending and larger surplus multi-engine aircraft were becoming available. The airlines would all capitalize on this innovation, which also saw the first flight attendants onboard Alaska's flights.

All of the ambitions, dreams and goals of a dozen small airline adventurers and entrepreneurs and their loyal employees would come together with the incorporation of Alaska Airlines. The days of heroic bush piloting were coming to an end, as were the days of being a water taxi service. The World War II veterans who made up many of the new airlines' employees would ensure not only Alaska's survival, but its triumph as a major airline.

(*top*) In 1944, the Alaska Star Airlines logo became the new Alaska Airlines simply by painting over the letters STAR. This logo on the side of a Lockheed Orion is a good example.

(*bottom*) An Alaska Airlines Bellanca Skyrocket is tied down outside the airline's hangar and ticket office at Merrill Field in Anchorage.

Kenny Gilchrist in his
instrument shop

John Penning

Ruben Stenderson

Alaska Airlines employees working at Merrill Field in Anchorage, just after World War II.

(*previous page top left*) Kenny Gilchrist in the airline's instrument shop.

(*previous page top right*) Mechanic, cigarette in mouth, repairs a Lockheed Vega engine.

(*previous page bottom left*) Alaska Airlines radio operator John Penning utilizes one of the airline's only sources of communication.

(*previous page bottom right*) Early aircraft were made with wooden frames, seats and propellers. Ruben Steaderson checks wood supplies in the Merrill Field carpenter shop.

(*this page top*) In the late 1940s, a combination of old cars, including a Woody, sit outside Alaska Airlines' Hangar No. 1 at Merrill Field in Anchorage.

(*this page middle*) This hand-painted sign hung outside Alaska Airlines' Anchorage City Ticket Office in 1944. The word "Star" has been painted out of the logo, leaving Alaska off-center.

(*this page bottom*) A Fairchild Pilgrim sits on skis in the snow while its cargo is unloaded at Merrill Field. Bush pilots liked the elevated pilot's seat area, which gave them great visibility. This aircraft was in service as early as 1932 and used by Alaska Airlines into the 1940s.

A mechanic services an Alaska Airlines Stinson Reliant on the wet, dirt hangar apron in Nome.

(top) At the delivery of the first Douglas DC-3 in 1945 (from left): Harry Playford, Raymond Marshall and Ted Law. Marshall bought Alaska Star Airlines in 1942 and two years later incorporated it as Alaska Airlines. Law, born into an oil family, invested $250,000 in Alaska Star Airlines in 1943. He was the airline's president when the name was changed, becoming the first president of Alaska Airlines.

(bottom) Mechanics push a Fairchild Pilgrim past an Alaska Airlines DC-3 into the hangar at Paine Field in Everett, Washington, symbolizing the change from bush to modern airline.

The Starliner Era
1945 - 1955

Alaska Airlines began to blossom as World War II came to an end. The airline purchased several surplus Douglas DC-3s, DC-4s and Curtiss-Wright C-46s, all christened as "Starliners." It was an optimistic time in the country and for the airline, which moved from bush flying into larger aircraft. Passenger service to the Territory of Alaska's remote communities grew, as well, when Alaska Airlines became the first carrier to fly DC-3s equipped with skis. This resulted in a government contract to fly supplies and personnel to the Naval Petroleum Reserve (PET-4) in the remote northern Arctic.

James Wooten, a charismatic, dynamic businessman, became president in 1947. Wooten had made a name for himself with cargo operations at American Airlines and did the same for Alaska Airlines. In addition to expanding its successful regional cargo operation, he began a worldwide charter service that included participating in the Berlin Airlift, flying the first Anchorage-to-Hawaii flights, evacuating Chinese Nationalist forces during the Communist Revolution, and airlifting 40,000 Jews from Yemen

to Israel in "Operation Magic Carpet." In little more than a year, Alaska Airlines became the largest charter carrier in the world. It was also showing a nice profit, and the airline moved its base from Merrill Field in Anchorage to Paine Field, north of Seattle.

The worldwide flying was short-lived, however, when the government's Civil Aeronautics Board (CAB) tightened its regulations, causing James Wooten to leave the company. In 1951, the CAB also took owner Raymond W. Marshall to task for his unusual business practices, forcing him to put his stock in a voting trust. With Marshall's influence weakened, the CAB put new professional management in place, including Nelson "Nels" David as president. He had the board of directors approve permanent corporate headquarters to be established at 2320 Sixth Avenue, Seattle, Washington, on June 5, 1953. Alaska Airlines also celebrated when the CAB gave it a permanent certificate to serve Portland-Seattle-Fairbanks-Anchorage routes in 1951. After trying for decades, the route from Alaska to the Lower 48 states was finally a reality.

(*top*) A champagne bottle bursts as it hits the engine propeller hub of the 21-seat Douglas DC-3 "Starliner Fairbanks," christening it into the Alaska Airlines fleet in May 1945. This aircraft carried 36 passengers and cruised at 167 mph.

(*bottom*) Alaska Airlines flight crews stand in front of two of the carrier's Douglas DC-3 "Starliners" in the late 1940s. These twin-engine World War II surplus aircraft were refurbished to become the pride and mainstay of the airline.

(*top*) *Alaska Airlines Collection*
(*bottom*) *Ron Suttell Collection*

(*top*) Alaska Airlines' first two flight attendants were hired in 1945 after the end of World War II. Maxine Branham (left) was from the Territory of Alaska and Renee Brust hailed from Detroit.

(*bottom*) In the late 1940s and 1950s, passengers would mingle on the tarmac before boarding an Alaska Airlines Douglas DC-3 "Starliner." DC-3s are legendary to this day, having opened the world and remote communities to aviation as a normal means of transportation.

(*next page*) A 1950s timetable, "Route of the Starliners," graphically shows the destinations reached by Alaska Airlines' DC-3s and DC-4s.

Ron Suttell Collection

FARES

One Way, Light face / Round Trip, Bold face	Anchorage	Aniak	Bethel	Fairbanks	Flat	Homer	Iliamna	Kenai	King Salmon	Kotzebue	McGrath	Nenana	Nome	Nyac	Portland	Seattle	Seldovia	Seward	Summit	Talkeetna	Unalakleet
ANCHORAGE		97.20	108.00	54.00	81.00	30.60	53.10	17.55	74.70	144.00	63.00	45.00	108.00	105.30	174.60	162.00	44.10	25.20	39.60	25.20	99.00
ANIAK	54.00		32.40		36.00						45.00			27.00	271.80	259.20					
BETHEL	60.00	18.00		135.00	54.00	105.30	99.00	108.00	72.00		63.00		135.00	27.00	282.60	270.00					122.40
FAIRBANKS	30.00		75.00			84.60	107.10	71.55	128.70		27.00	21.60			174.60	162.00			32.40	46.80	
FLAT	45.00	20.00	30.00											45.00	255.60	243.00					
HOMER	17.00		58.50	47.00			26.10	25.20	52.20		93.60	75.60	138.60		205.20	192.60		43.20	70.20	55.80	129.60
ILIAMNA	29.50		55.00	59.50		14.50		50.40	26.10		116.10	98.10	161.10		227.70	215.10			92.70	78.30	152.10
KENAI	9.75		60.00	39.75			14.00		28.00	74.70	80.55	62.55	125.55		192.15	179.75			57.15	42.75	116.55
KING SALMON	41.50		40.00	71.50			29.00	14.50		41.50					249.30	236.70			114.30	99.90	173.70
KOTZEBUE	80.00										108.00		45.00	81.00	318.60	306.00					63.00
McGRATH	35.00	25.00	35.00		15.00					60.00			129.60	54.00	219.60	207.00			45.00	54.00	122.40
NENANA	25.00			12.00		42.00	54.50	34.75	66.50		45.00		72.00								
NOME	60.00		75.00			77.00	89.50	69.75	101.50	25.00	45.00	30.00			279.90	267.30			147.60	133.20	54.00
NYAC	58.50	15.00	15.00		25.00						30.00										
PORTLAND	97.00	151.00	157.00	97.00	142.00	114.00	126.50	106.75	138.50	177.00	132.00	122.00	157.00	155.50			218.70	199.80	214.20	199.80	273.60
SEATTLE	90.00	144.00	150.00	90.00	135.00	107.00	119.50	99.75	131.50	170.00	125.00	115.00	150.00	148.50			206.10	182.20	201.60	187.20	261.00
SELDOVIA	24.50														121.50	114.50		56.70			
SEWARD	14.00					24.00									111.00	104.00	31.50				
SUMMIT	22.00					39.00	51.50	31.75	63.50			25.00	82.00		119.00	112.00				25.20	
TALKEETNA	14.00			26.00		31.00	43.50	23.75	55.50			30.00	74.00		111.00	104.00			14.00		
UNALAKLEET	55.00		68.00			72.00	84.50	64.75	96.50	50.00	35.00	68.00	30.00		152.00	145.00					

GENERAL INFORMATION

CHILDREN'S FARES—A child in arms under two years of age will be carried free when accompanied by parent or guardian and provided parent or guardian has paid effective fare. Children under 12 years of age one-half fare.

CHARTER RATES—Between various points are available. For information contact your nearest Alaska Airlines Office.

BAGGAGE—Fifty-five (55) pounds of baggage will be carried free on each ticket within the Territory of Alaska. Sixty-six (66) pounds of baggage will be carried free on each ticket between Alaska points and the United States and International points. Baggage over the allowable limit will be charged for at the rate per pound of one-half of one percent of the one-way fare with a minimum charge of twenty-five cents.

TIMETABLES—These timetables show the times at which planes may be expected to depart from and arrive at the stations shown, but are subject to change without notice and are not guaranteed.

FREIGHT RATES—17 cents per pound per 100 lbs. weight applicable to both Fairbanks and Anchorage from Seattle and Portland. Special commodity rates to Fairbanks only. For further freight information including intra Alaska freight rates and service please contact your nearest Alaska Airlines Freight Office.

EQUIPMENT—Douglas DC-3 21-passenger or DC-4 Starliners with Stewardess service on all Douglas Schedules.

CHARTER SERVICE — FOUR-ENGINE DC-4 "STARLINERS" — TWIN ENGINE DC-3 AND CURTIS C-46's AS WELL AS SINGLE ENGINE AIRCRAFT ARE AVAILABLE FOR ALL TYPES OF PLEASURE OR BUSINESS TRIPS. FOR INFORMATION CONTACT YOUR NEAREST ALASKA AIRLINES OFFICE.

T & S. No. 2.

(top) Alaska Airlines Collection
(bottom) Don "Bucky" Dawson Collection: Keith T. Petrich Photo

(*previous page top*) A flight attendant helps load cargo into a Douglas DC-3 through the doorway just behind the cockpit in the late 1940s. Often used on frozen, snow-covered runways, Alaska Airlines' DC-3s were the first certified by the FAA to operate on skis.

(*previous page bottom*) Three twin-engine Curtiss C-46 "Starliners" sit along a melting runway at Weeks Field in Fairbanks. In May of 1948, Alaska Airlines flew a C-46 out of Shanghai Airport, which became the last commercial flight before Communists took possession of the airport.

(*previous page wings*)
Captain Stan Baumwald Collection
Alaska Airlines flight attendants wore half wings on their uniforms in the late 1940s and 1950s.

(*above*) A dog team delivers cargo to an Alaska Airlines Curtiss C-46 in the late 1940s. Called the "Commando," this aircraft was renowned in World War II for moving material to every front and for flying "The Hump," the famed route over the Himalayas, to deliver critical supplies to Chinese allies.

R-2000 ENGINE TEARDOWN - NOTE SPECIAL TOOLS ON PARTS RACK - ENGINE OVERHAUL SHOP - PAINE FIELD

TIME TABLE

ALASKA AIRLINES

Route of the Starliners

SERVING ALL ALASKA

ALASKA AIRLINES

FINAL ASSEMBLY LINE - ENGINE OVERHAUL SHOP - PAINE FIELD

(both top) Ron Suttell Collection: Juleen Studio Photos (bottom) Ron Suttell Collection

(*top left*) Two mechanics work on an R-200 engine in the overhaul shop at Paine Field in Everett, Washington, in 1948.

(*top right*) Concentrated activity on the final assembly line at the Paine Field engine overhaul shop.

(*timetable*) A colorful 1950s timetable showcases the four-engines on a Douglas DC-4 as it advertises the "Route of the Starliners."

(*bottom*) Mechanics work on a Douglas DC-4, the "Starliner Matanuska," at Paine Field in the early 1950s.

(sticker) *Jeff Cacy Collection* An Alaska Airlines sticker from the early 1950s highlights the Starliner logo, Douglas DC-4 and Alaskan scenery.

.

(photo) A flight crew member helps load cargo into the Douglas DC-4 "Starliner Anchorage" in the early 1950s. Alaska Airlines purchased its first DC-4 in 1946 and began non-scheduled flights, both cargo and passenger, between Seattle and Anchorage in 1947. An Alaska Airlines DC-4 made the first commercial flight over the North Pole on December 12, 1951.

(top left) DC-4 First Officer Warren Metzger and Flight Attendant Marian Liscomb worked together on the Berlin airlift and married on January 24, 1949, when they were both involved in "Operation Magic Carpet."

(top middle) A publicity picture from the early 1950s shows an Alaska Airlines flight attendant and a young polar bear in transit to Seattle's Woodland Park Zoo.

(far right) Captain Gene Wheeler and Alaska Airlines passengers next to a Douglas DC-4.

(right) A pilot holds a Jewish child during "Operation Magic Carpet" in 1949. Alaska Airlines contracted to transport Yemenite Jews to the newly formed state of Israel.

(wings) Captain Stan Baumwald Collection
Alaska Airlines pilot's hat wings in the late 1940s.

ALASKA AIRLINES

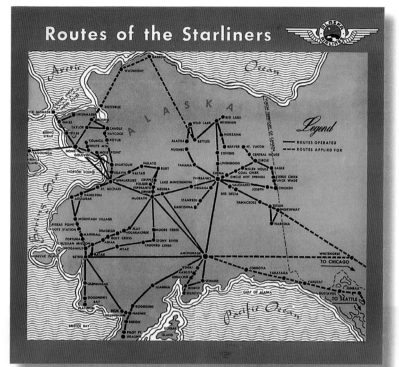

Routes of the Starliners

Legend
— ROUTES OPERATED
---- ROUTES APPLIED FOR

(both top) Alaska Airlines Collection
(bottom) Ron Suttell Collection

(*top left*) A BMW Isetta is loaded into an Alaska Airlines Douglas DC-4. The airline was operating contract services between London, Johannesburg, Mexico City and Madrid in 1948.

(*top right*) This late 1947 route map features the non-scheduled and connecting routes Alaska Airlines flew to Seattle, Minneapolis and Chicago. The airline was also flying routes throughout the Territory of Alaska, and was awarded a scheduled route to Seattle in 1951.

(*bottom*) Alaska Airlines operated five Bell 47B helicopters to service North Slope oil exploration in 1949 and 1950, becoming the first airline in Alaska to use rotary-wing aircraft. This helicopter is about to land at Merrill Field in Anchorage.

Alaska Island Airlines, Inc.

1946 - 1951

Alaska Island Airways was formed as a corporation in 1946 in Alaska's "Little Norway," the town of Petersburg. The investors were Clarence E. "Slim" Walters, Jim Noland, Carl Omdahl and George Brink. They bought Petersburg Air Service from Tony Schwamm, renaming it Alaska Island Airlines. The airline started with bases in Petersburg and Wrangell, which were also their main destinations. They tried unsuccessfully to get approval as a scheduled airline, so they operated on a charter basis in the area.

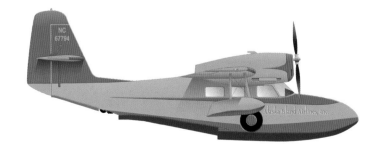

Captain William Stedman Collection
Alaska Island Airlines flew the Grumman Widgeon aircraft for nearly 10 years, servicing Southeast Alaska communities from its base at Petersburg Airport.

Alaska Coastal Airlines purchased the aircraft and the airline's lucrative Petersburg and Wrangell bases in 1951. Walters, one of Alaska Island Airlines' investors who had also flown for Ellis Air Transport, and pilot Dave Brown, along with mechanic-pilot Bill Stedman went to work for Shell Simmons at Alaska Coastal in Juneau. One of Alaska Island Airlines pilots, Jim Hickey Jr., joined Bob Ellis at Ellis Air Lines.

Alaska Island Airlines flew three Cabin Wacos and two Grumman Widgeons, all amphibious aircraft, which were painted a flashy international orange and bright yellow. At its peak, Alaska Island Airlines employed six pilots.

When Alaska Coastal-Ellis Airlines eventually merged with Alaska Airlines in 1968, the Alaska Island Airlines bases in Petersburg and Wrangell went with that agreement. The amphibious aircraft were replaced by DeHavilland DHC-6 Twin Otters and, eventually, today's modern Boeing jets, but the spirit of those early Southeast aviation pioneers lives on at Alaska Airlines.

Collins Air Service

1947 - 1950

Grenold Collins became a noted bush pilot in the early 1940s, mostly to make his jobs easier as a game warden and later a wildlife agent for the U.S. Bureau of Biological Survey. As a result of his travels in Alaska, Collins also became an avid hunter and wildlife photographer. Over the years, he created a huge archive of hunting and bush flying photos, and movies of Alaskan, Canadian, Asian and African subjects.

Museum of Flight Seattle: Robert W. Stevens Collection
Dressed in winter furs, Collins Air Service founder Glen Collins stands next to Frank Glaser in front of the airline's Piper 3F-50.

Collins was born in Tacoma, Washington, in 1907 and educated at prep schools there and in California before attending Stanford and the University of Washington. He worked at various jobs in Washington, Nevada and California and finally arrived in Alaska, where he began his flying career with the U.S. government. Collins also flew for construction firm Morrison-Knudsen during World War II.

After the war, he decided to strike out on his own, founding Gren Collins Charter Airplane and Big Game Guide Service, based on Kodiak Island. At the same time, he served in the Alaska Territorial Senate and was the Western Alaska representative of the Salmon Division of the Libby McNeil Company. The airline's name was shortened to Collins Air Service in 1947, mostly to save space on paper work, according to his wife, Dorothy Booth Tibbs. Together they also owned a treasure shop and the Global Travel Agency in Anchorage. Alaska Airlines purchased Collins Air Service in 1950, primarily to acquire its Kodiak routes.

University of Alaska Fairbanks: Kay J. Kennedy Collection

A man looks out of the forward hatch of a Collins Air Service Grumman Goose on a rocky runway on Kodiak Island.

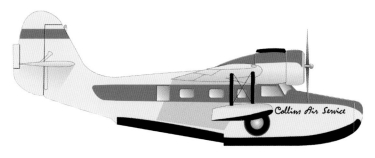

ALASKA AIRLINES

The Golden Eagle Era
1955 - 1966

The 1950s were a time of innovation at Alaska Airlines. Capitalizing on its new routes between Alaska, Seattle and Portland, the carrier added larger Douglas DC-6 pressurized planes, enabling flights above the clouds and harsh weather. Alaska also purchased three workhorse Lockheed Constellations, the longest-ranged piston aircraft ever built, to boost worldwide cargo operations. During this busy time, Alaska also purchased two small airlines, Collins Air Service of Kodiak and Al Jones Airways of Bethel, expanding the route system. The new aircraft adopted a Golden Eagle tail logo, which remains on today's pilot and flight attendant wings.

The Civil Aeronautics Board (CAB) appointed Nelson David as president in 1952, and he began to improve Alaska's financial stability. Still not free of R.W. Marshall, however, David resigned in May of 1957. The CAB forced Marshall to sell his majority stock, and he did so to a politically connected World War II Navy hero, Charles F. Willis Jr., who became Alaska's new president and first CEO.

Willis was a colorful marketer who introduced a new spark to inflight services, setting them apart from other carriers. On DC-6 flights, a small bar was created, complete with a piano and "free beer" tap. The food was upgraded, and a movie projector and music sound system were installed. These early innovations were the beginning of the airline's reputation for superior passenger service that continues today. It was a good time for Alaska Airlines as well as the Territory of Alaska, which became the 49th state on January 3, 1959.

Alaska Airlines purchased its first Douglas DC-6A in 1958, a year
before Alaska statehood. The aircraft was the pride of the fleet
for a time, flying mainline routes and charters around the world.

GULF OF ALASKA

BERING SEA

ALASKA
AIRLINES
ROUTE OF THE STARLINERS

SEATTLE

PORTLAND

(*left*) A 1950s Starliners route map, which overlapped with the new Golden Eagle paint scheme, shows the regularly scheduled route from the Territory of Alaska to Seattle and Portland.

(*wings*) *Captain Dick Adams Family Collection*
Alaska Airlines pilot's wings worn in the late 1950s and into the 1960s.

(*bottom*) Alaska Airlines flight attendant Julie Sparks pulls the beer tap onboard a DC-6. President Charlie Willis had the bar installed and served free beer to all military personnel.

(*left*) *Ron Suttell Collection*
(*right*) *Alaska Airlines Collection*

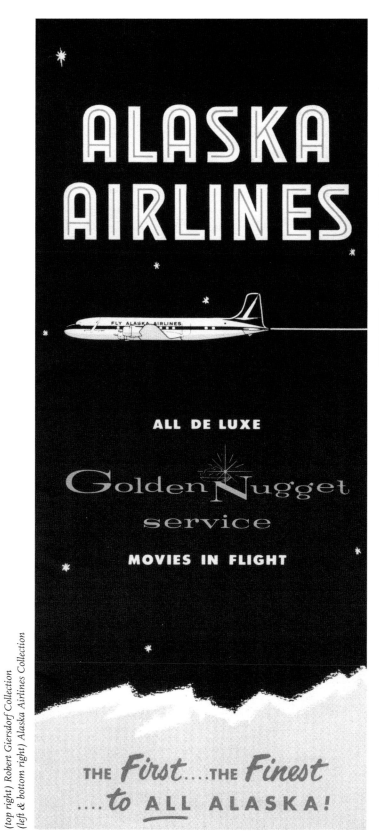

ALASKA AIRLINES

FLY ALASKA AIRLINES

ALL DE LUXE

Golden Nugget
service

MOVIES IN FLIGHT

THE *First*....THE *Finest*
....*to* ALL ALASKA!

(*left*) A 1960 Alaska Airlines brochure advertised "Golden Nugget Service" and in-flight movies onboard the Golden Eagle Douglas DC-6C.

(*top right*) The first movie shown onboard an Alaska Airlines DC-6 was a Jerry Lewis comedy. Unfortunately, the movie was not prescreened and it opened with a 1935 newspaper headline that read: "Will Rogers, Wiley Post Die in Alaska Air Crash."

(*bottom right*) An Alaska Airlines Douglas DC-6C is parked at Seattle-Tacoma Airport. It was the airline's first pressurized aircraft and flew the Seattle-Fairbanks-Anchorage route in 1958.

This is to certify that

_____

is a fully accredited, lifetime member in the

ARCTIC CIRCLE CLUB

having crossed the Arctic Circle, Territory of

Alaska, at _____ North Latitude

and _____ West Longitude

at _____ M., Bering Sea Time, as a

passenger on Alaska Airlines Flight No. _____

from _____ to _____

an _____

ALASKA AIRLINES

Charlie Willis

PRESIDENT & GENERAL MANAGER

PILOT IN COMMAND

(*previous page photo*) An Alaska Airlines Lockheed L-1649 Starliner Constellation sits beside a frozen runway at Indian Mountain Air Force Station, a radar site 165 miles northwest of Fairbanks. In the early 1960s, Alaska had a government military contract to haul supplies to high-security cold war outposts.

(*previous page certificate*) Beginning in the late 1950s, every passenger crossing the Arctic Circle received a special certificate signed by Alaska Airlines President Charlie Willis.

(*above*) Captain Warren Metzger photographed this dramatic takeoff of an Alaska Airlines Lockheed Constellation L-1049 "Super Connie" at Nome in 1962. The airline leased Super Constellations for cargo and passenger service, and placed them on Anchorage, Seattle, Nome and Kotzebue flights.

(top left) Captain Dick Adams Family Collection
(top right) Robert Giersdorf Collection
(bottom) Captain Chuck & Gail Spaeth Collection

(*top left*) In fur ruffs and golden velvet jackets, Alaska Airlines flight attendants Penny Plato (left) and Karel "Kay" Donnelly smile for the camera in this 1960s photo.

(*top right*) An Alaska Airlines flight attendant serves meals in the 1960s.

(*bottom*) Ground crews work on an Alaska Airlines Lockheed Starliner parked at Anchorage Airport. Two L-1649 Starliners, the longest-range piston airliners ever built, were used as all-cargo transports, along with one smaller 1049H Super Constellation.

Captain Dick Adams Family Collection

(photo) An Alaska Airlines flight crew poses in the late 1960s (from left): Flight Attendant Chris Hall, First Officer Chuck Spaeth, Flight Attendant Marilyn Moffet, Captain Dick Adams and Flight Attendant Mardra Jones (famous musician and record producer Quincy Jones' sister).

(hat) *Captain Dick Adams Family Collection.* Alaska Airlines captain's wings and hat worn in the late 1950s and into the 1960s.

The Jet Age
1961

As statehood roared into Alaska so did the tourists. Alaska Airlines went after this lucrative market by promoting itself heavily and organizing charters from the smaller states to "Alaska's Frozen Far North." The carrier conducted a promotional tour of Japan in an effort to attract visitors from Asia and began building a unique identity over the Alaska-Seattle route. Competing airlines saw this growth in traffic and started flying jets on the route.

With no money to buy jet aircraft, Alaska Airlines President Charlie Willis displayed his marketing skills by talking General Dynamics into selling the airline a new Convair 880 jet with nothing down. Delivery of the new aircraft in August 1961 caused something of a sensation, setting a Los Angeles-to-Seattle passenger jet record of one hour and forty three minutes — which still stands today.

Since Alaska Airlines only had the one jet, they came up with a new type of maintenance program to keep it constantly flying.

Some part of the jet would be overhauled every day. The Federal Aviation Agency (now the Federal Aviation Administration) agreed to this phased maintenance program, an innovation that is used throughout the industry now. The aircraft featured modified two- and three-seat coach accommodations, with all first class service. This gave the airline the opportunity to promote a comfortable ride with better food and service.

Boeing then introduced its new 727 jets and Alaska Airlines quickly moved to the more efficient aircraft beginning in 1966. The sleek Boeing jet would become the carrier's signature aircraft for the next 25 years. During this period of growth, the airline relinquished many of its bush routes to tiny towns in the interior of Alaska, focusing on the longer and more profitable routes. Competition was tough, but Alaska Airlines once again struck promotional gold with the introduction of its "Golden Nugget" service.

In July 1961, Alaska Airlines took possession of its first jetliner, this 96-seat Convair 880, pictured flying by Mount McKinley. The aircraft reduced the flying time between Seattle and Fairbanks from six hours to three.

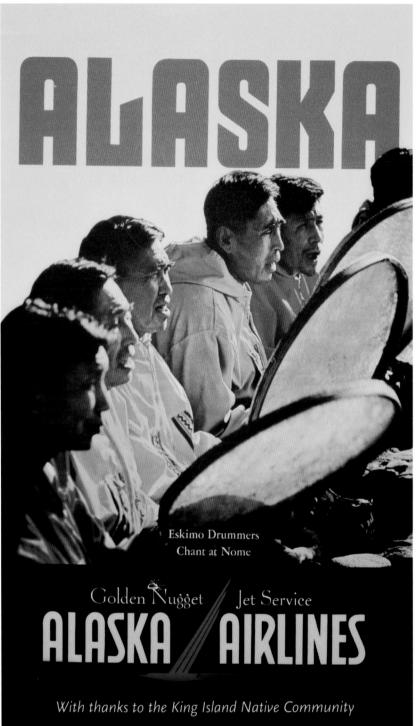

(*left*) This beautiful photograph of an Eskimo mother and child, along with the image of a seal-skin drum, was used for advertising from the late 1950s into the mid 1960s.

(*right*) Nome's King Island Eskimo Drummers are featured in this poster, which Alaska Airlines used to promote its new Convair 880 jet service.

(both) Jack & David Bates Collection: Bob & Ira Spring Photos

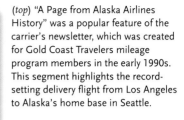

A PAGE FROM
ALASKA AIRLINES HISTORY

Alaska Airlines Sets a New Flight Speed Record

Murals of Alaska scenery graced the Convair's roomy First Class lounge.

It was 5:00 p.m. on July 31, 1961, when a shining white jet emblazoned with a stylized golden eagle took off from Los Angeles. Only one hour and forty-three minutes later, the plane and its passengers arrived in Seattle—a new commercial flight speed record! This historic trip was the delivery flight for Alaska Airlines first jet, the Convair 880. According to Jon Proctor, who just finished a book on the Convair, "the Convair 880 was comfortable, quiet, and most of all, fast. Alaska Airlines made the most of the Convair with daily service between Seattle and Alaska, however, the plane used a lot of fuel and had limited passenger and cargo capacity. When the more efficient Boeing 727 came within Alaska's reach in 1966, the airline made the change." • Today, Alaska Airlines operates more than 75 jets daily and makes the more customary two and one half hour LAX to Seattle flight fifteen times a day!

Alaska's Convair also set a speed record between Seattle and Fairbanks with a 2 hour 22 minute one-way flight!

(top) "A Page from Alaska Airlines History" was a popular feature of the carrier's newsletter, which was created for Gold Coast Travelers mileage program members in the early 1990s. This segment highlights the record-setting delivery flight from Los Angeles to Alaska's home base in Seattle.

(bottom) Alaska Airlines' first Convair 880 parked on the tarmac at Seattle-Tacoma International Airport.

(*left*) Alaska Airlines Flight Attendant Micki Bliss works in the galley of the Convair 880 in the early 1960s.

(*next page brochure*) This 1963 Alaska Airlines brochure shows the Convair 880 flying above a typical Southeast Alaska scene. The aircraft was painted in the Golden Eagle scheme and advertised as the Golden Nugget Jet.

(*next page photo*) In-flight service in the first class lounge of the Convair 880 was elaborate, with Flight Attendant Micki Bliss serving an impressive appetizer tray. Colorful Alaskan scenes were painted on the cabin walls and the middle of the coach section featured a draft beer bar.

(*both pages*) *Alaska Airlines Collection*

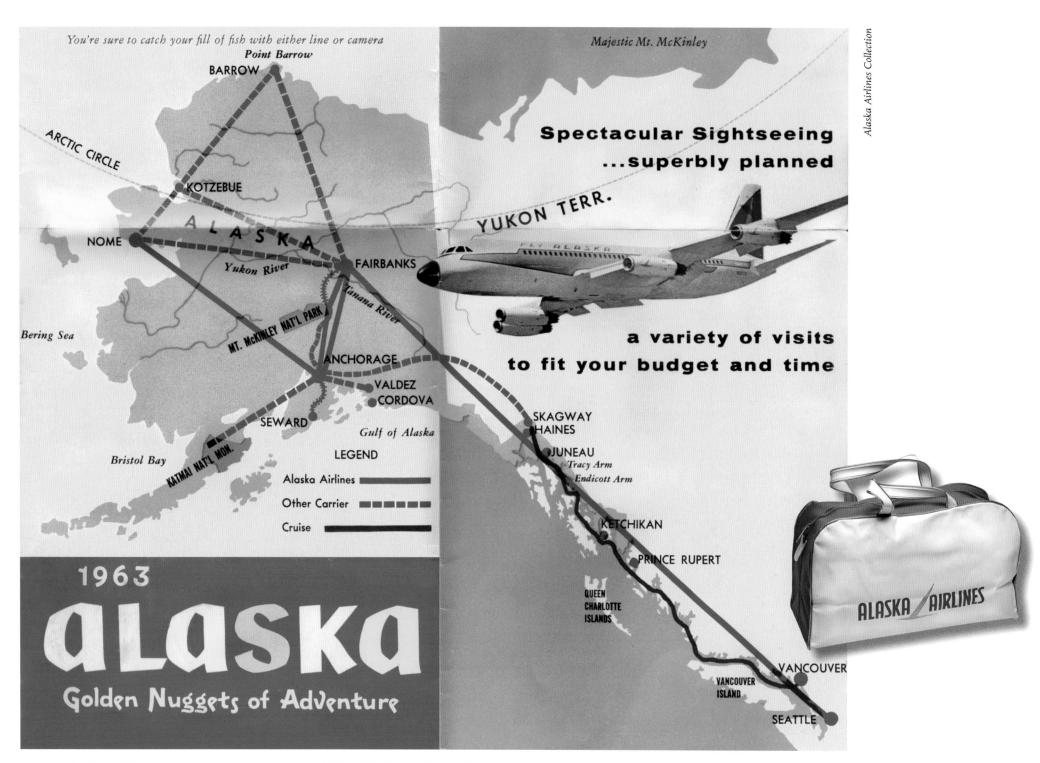

You're sure to catch your fill of fish with either line or camera

Majestic Mt. McKinley

Point Barrow
BARROW

ARCTIC CIRCLE

KOTZEBUE

A L A S K A

NOME

Yukon River

FAIRBANKS

Tanana River

Bering Sea

MT. McKINLEY NAT'L PARK

ANCHORAGE

VALDEZ
CORDOVA

SEWARD

Bristol Bay

KATMAI NAT'L MON.

Gulf of Alaska

LEGEND

Alaska Airlines ————
Other Carrier – – – –
Cruise ————

1963
ALASKA
Golden Nuggets of Adventure

Spectacular Sightseeing
...superbly planned

YUKON TERR.

a variety of visits
to fit your budget and time

SKAGWAY
HAINES

JUNEAU
Tracy Arm
Endicott Arm

KETCHIKAN

PRINCE RUPERT

QUEEN
CHARLOTTE
ISLANDS

VANCOUVER

VANCOUVER
ISLAND

SEATTLE

ALASKA AIRLINES

(*above*) Alaska Airlines' 1963 route map was cleverly designed to make Fairbanks and Anchorage appear to be an equal distance from Seattle. Since the airline did not have a direct flight between Seattle and Anchorage, the map made it seem less of a disadvantage to fly via Fairbanks.

(*bag*) *Jeff Cacy Collection.* The Alaska Airlines flight bags of the 1960s featured the Golden Eagle design and the red, white and gold colors of the aircraft.

(*above*) An Alaska Airlines Convair 880 is parked at the terminal at Seattle-Tacoma International Airport. This aircraft was configured to carry 96 passengers at speeds much faster than the DC-6.

(*illustration*) *Bryant Petitt, Artist*. Always looking for ways to compete with larger carriers, Alaska Airlines ran a billboard in Seattle, similar to this illustration, promoting their "Four Jets" daily to Anchorage. The clever wording concealed that the four jets were on a single aircraft operating one flight a day between the two cities.

ALASKA
Coastal-Ellis
AIRLINES

1962 - 1968

The merger of two successful Southeast Alaskan competitors, Alaska Coastal and Ellis Air Lines, created Alaska Coastal-Ellis Airlines on April Fool's Day of 1962. Both carriers had been growth restricted because of their location, and the merger provided the size and strength needed to create a strong bargaining position when larger airlines looked to expand.

Alaska Coastal-Ellis was well matched, with large fleets of amphibious aircraft, extensive route systems and a group of nearly 500 loyal employees. For a time, they were the largest airline in the state of Alaska, with the highest passenger-per-route-mile average of any carrier.

Alaska Coastal-Ellis was ideal for serving an area with no roads connecting the major cities — although, at the time of the merger, Ketchikan, Sitka, Wrangell, Petersburg and the state capital in Juneau were beginning to improve their land-based airport systems. In less than five years, several of these cities were also being served sporadically by wheel-equipped planes, making those routes a valuable commodity for a possible merger. Alaska Airlines, with its extensive intrastate route system and connections to the Lower 48 states, seemed the ideal match for this still-young airline.

After operating for six years, Alaska Coastal-Ellis merged with Alaska Airlines in 1968. Sheldon "Shell" Simmons had said about the Coastal-Ellis merger, "We pledge this airline — built by Alaskans, financed by Alaskans and operated by Alaskans — will always be Alaska's Finest Airline." Now "Alaska's Finest" would become an essential part of the Spirit of Alaska Airlines. Simmons and Bob Ellis joined Alaska's Board of Directors, as did their manager, Ben Benecke, who later served as the president of Alaska Airlines. Many outstanding Alaska Coastal-Ellis employees have retired from Alaska Airlines.

An Alaska Coastal-Ellis Grumman Goose, hoisted from Ketchikan waters. The aircraft featured two different engines. The older one is being changed to a more powerful and efficient turbine engine, which was later dubbed the "Turbo Goose." A smaller Cessna 185D sits next to the dock below.

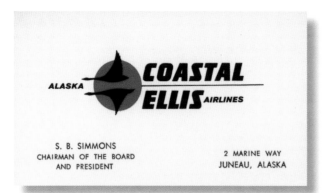

(photo) A mechanic works on an Alaska Coastal-Ellis Grumman Goose tied to a dock in Ketchikan, Alaska. When Alaska Coastal and Ellis Air Lines merged, their combined aircraft fleet consisted of four PBY Catalinas and 17 Grumman Goose amphibians.

Mary Goodwin Collection

(*photo*) An Alaska Coastal-Ellis Grumman Goose
takes off in front of Mendenhall Glacier, near Juneau.

(*patch*) *Captain Stan Baumwald Collection*
Alaska Coastal-Ellis pilot's embroidered wings.

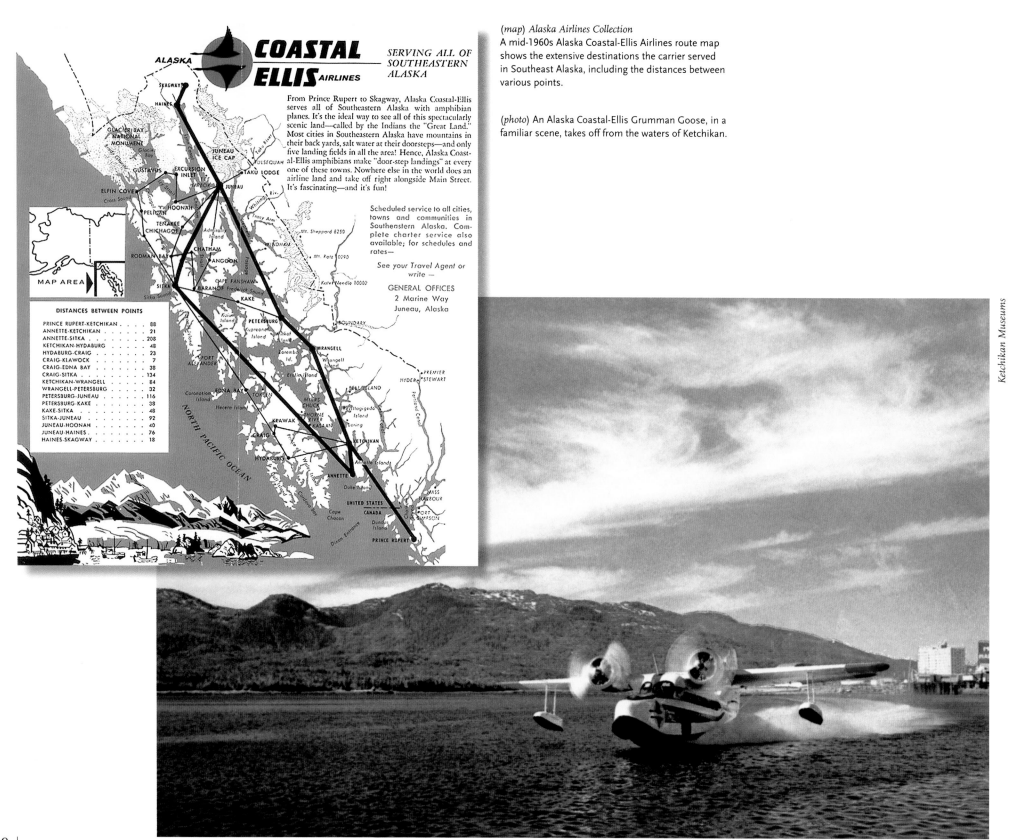

COASTAL ELLIS AIRLINES

SERVING ALL OF SOUTHEASTERN ALASKA

From Prince Rupert to Skagway, Alaska Coastal-Ellis serves all of Southeastern Alaska with amphibian planes. It's the ideal way to see all of this spectacularly scenic land—called by the Indians the "Great Land." Most cities in Southeastern Alaska have mountains in their back yards, salt water at their doorsteps—and only five landing fields in all the area! Hence, Alaska Coastal-Ellis amphibians make "door-step landings" at every one of these towns. Nowhere else in the world does an airline land and take off right alongside Main Street. It's fascinating—and it's fun!

Scheduled service to all cities, towns and communities in Southeastern Alaska. Complete charter service also available; for schedules and rates—

See your Travel Agent or write —

GENERAL OFFICES
2 Marine Way
Juneau, Alaska

DISTANCES BETWEEN POINTS

PRINCE RUPERT-KETCHIKAN	88
ANNETTE-KETCHIKAN	21
ANNETTE-SITKA	208
KETCHIKAN-HYDABURG	48
HYDABURG-CRAIG	23
CRAIG-KLAWOCK	7
CRAIG-EDNA BAY	38
CRAIG-SITKA	134
KETCHIKAN-WRANGELL	84
WRANGELL-PETERSBURG	32
PETERSBURG-JUNEAU	116
PETERSBURG-KAKE	38
KAKE-SITKA	48
SITKA-JUNEAU	92
JUNEAU-HOONAH	40
JUNEAU-HAINES	76
HAINES-SKAGWAY	18

(map) *Alaska Airlines Collection*
A mid-1960s Alaska Coastal-Ellis Airlines route map shows the extensive destinations the carrier served in Southeast Alaska, including the distances between various points.

(photo) An Alaska Coastal-Ellis Grumman Goose, in a familiar scene, takes off from the waters of Ketchikan.

Ketchikan Museums

Terry Richards Collection

SCHEDULED AND CHARTER SERVICES
TO ALL SOUTHEASTERN
ALASKA AND PRINCE RUPERT, B.C

Reservations and Information

Angoon	788-3131
Annette	882-5111
Craig	285-3132
Haines	766-3131
Hoonah	945-3111
Hydaburg	826-3314
Juneau	586-2205
Kake	785-3121
Ketchikan	CA5-2141
Klawock	826-3233
Pelican	735-4221
Petersburg	772-4518
Prince Rupert	624-2223
Skagway	YU3-2211
Sitka	747-3211
Wrangell	844-3412

ALASKA COASTAL AIRLINES

SCHEDULES

going your way in scenic Southeastern ALASKA

fly with **ALASKA COASTAL AIRLINES**

2 Marine Way   Juneau, Alaska

(*above*) Reflected in the smooth waters of Behm Canal near Old Bell Island Health Springs in Southeast Alaska, an Alaska Coastal-Ellis Grumman Goose is tied to a handmade dock. These amphibious aircraft brought the outside world to isolated Alaska communities.

(*timetable*) *Ron Suttell Collection*
Alaska Coastal Airlines printed this schedule in the late 1960s.

The Golden Nugget Era
1966 - 1972

Alaska Airlines took delivery of its first Boeing 727-90C in October of 1966, with interiors decorated in the Gold Rush Gay '90s style, and so began the Golden Nugget Era. Airline President Charlie Willis wanted his passengers to have "an experience, not just a trip." He changed the cabin design, authorized flight attendant uniforms that looked like Edwardian costumes, and had them perform fashion shows in the aisles. Bingo games were also staged en route.

Business improved so Charlie Willis began to make purchases that would change the dynamics of the airline. Alaska Airlines bought the North Star Hotel in Nome and then Alyeska Ski Resort near Anchorage. Flights were expanded in Southeast Alaska with jet service to Sitka, and Alaska Coastal-Ellis and Cordova Airlines were purchased. Alaska Airlines received Federal Aviation Administration approval for Boeing 727 jets to land and take off from dirt and gravel runways. Alaska was the first airline allowed to make gravel landings with jets.

Willis learned that Atlantic Richfield planned to drill on the state's North Slope. They would need to transport tons of equipment, so he bargained for a C-130 Hercules aircraft from Lockheed with no money down, and Alaska Airlines became the first commercial operator of the "Hercs." After proving the feasibility of flying heavy loads into remote areas, Texaco and Mobil hired Alaska Airlines to transport drilling rigs into South America. More Hercs were leased and flights began moving freight all over the world, including military supplies into the Vietnam War.

Money problems didn't stop Willis and his marketing genius, Bob Giersdorf. The company operated on the verge of bankruptcy in 1972 as the Golden Nugget Era came to an end. While it was fun and exciting, nervous employees wanted more financial security and wondered what was next for the venturesome airline.

SKIING IS TOPS AT THE TOP OF THE WORLD

Mt. Alyeska
Alaska

Ski Alyeska

via **ALASKA** AIRLINES

GOLDEN NUGGET JETS

Take a glorious ski vacation in Alaska for as little as $25.00 down.

(*photo*) Alaska Airlines' first Boeing 727-90C gave passengers a breathtaking view of Mount McKinley and the Alaska Range.

(*brochure*) *Ron Suttell Collection: Bob & Ira Spring Photo* Alyeska Ski Resort, located in Girdwood 40 miles from Anchorage, was owned for a time by Alaska Airlines and managed by European travel businessman Chris von Imhof. The cover shows Chris (*forward left*), and his wife, Nina, as they prepare to ski down the mountain.

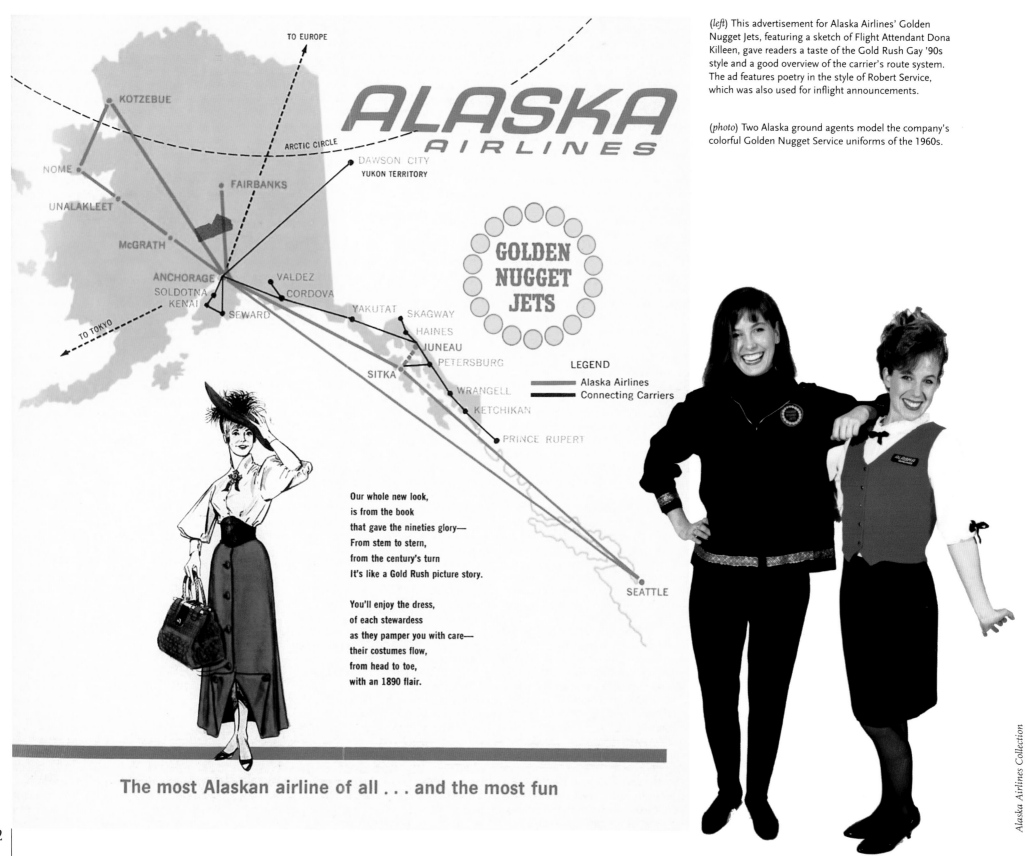

ALASKA AIRLINES

TO EUROPE

KOTZEBUE

ARCTIC CIRCLE

DAWSON CITY
YUKON TERRITORY

NOME

UNALAKLEET

FAIRBANKS

McGRATH

ANCHORAGE
SOLDOTNA
KENAI
SEWARD

VALDEZ
CORDOVA

TO TOKYO

YAKUTAT SKAGWAY
HAINES
JUNEAU
PETERSBURG

SITKA

WRANGELL

KETCHIKAN

PRINCE RUPERT

GOLDEN NUGGET JETS

LEGEND
▬▬ Alaska Airlines
▬▬ Connecting Carriers

SEATTLE

Our whole new look,
is from the book
that gave the nineties glory—
From stem to stern,
from the century's turn
It's like a Gold Rush picture story.

You'll enjoy the dress,
of each stewardess
as they pamper you with care—
their costumes flow,
from head to toe,
with an 1890 flair.

The most Alaskan airline of all . . . and the most fun

(*left*) This advertisement for Alaska Airlines' Golden Nugget Jets, featuring a sketch of Flight Attendant Dona Killeen, gave readers a taste of the Gold Rush Gay '90s style and a good overview of the carrier's route system. The ad features poetry in the style of Robert Service, which was also used for inflight announcements.

(*photo*) Two Alaska ground agents model the company's colorful Golden Nugget Service uniforms of the 1960s.

air travel

PART 2

News Supplement of **OFFICIAL AIRLINE GUIDE**   MAY, 1967

(*top left*) Flying over the Seattle area in 1966 is the first of three Alaska Airlines Boeing 727-90C Golden Nugget Jets. The aircraft had a main-cabin cargo door that allowed options for passengers and cargo.

(*bottom left*) Alaska Airlines purchased the North Star Hotel in Nome in 1966, changing its name to the Nugget Inn. The airline had extensive properties in Nome, eventually operating three "Nugget Inn" hotels to accommodate its Arctic tour packages, before selling them in the late 1970s.

(*right*) The *Official Airline Guide Supplement* provides a colorful glimpse at the simulated Gold Rush Gay '90s interior of an Alaska Airlines Boeing 727-90C. Built by the airline's mechanics on a Ford flatbed, this traveling promotional van toured the country during 1967. Annie Boshier (pictured) was one of flight attendants who "flew" the sales van.

FEATURED THIS MONTH:

(left) The December 1966 system schedule for Alaska Airlines' Golden Nugget Jets showcased the swinging saloon doors that were the entrance to the office of President Charlie Willis, and advertised its status as official airline of the Alaska State Centennial in 1967.

(center) Frank Feeman, Alaska Airlines' director of interline and agency sales, in his official Golden Nugget uniform.

(right) No. 1 in seniority today, Flight Attendant Judy White-Buchanan delivers food to passengers in her Alaska Airlines Golden Nugget uniform in the late 1960s. Bob Giersdorf, vice president of marketing, smiles at her from his aisle seat three rows back.

(slide rule) Alaska Airlines Collection
This circular aviation slide rule was used by Alaska Airlines flight crews on the Boeing 727 to calculate weight and balance.

Charlie Willis was only 38 and a decorated World War II Navy pilot when he was named president and the first chief executive officer of Alaska Airlines by R.W. Marshall. He served from 1957 to 1972, ordering three 727-100s from Boeing in 1964. All three jets were C models, built primarily as "combi" aircraft to accommodate passengers and cargo.

Willis had them delivered with the passenger compartment decorated in the Golden Nugget Gay '90s theme. Pictured in this photo for a sales promotion in Fairbanks are: driver Homer Mackey (owner of M&O Auto Parts and antique car collector), Gladys Chase, Kathy Hutchison and an unidentified passenger.

(*photo*) Parked in front of a Cordova hangar, this Alaska Airlines Golden Nugget Convair 240 was originally a Cordova Airlines aircraft acquired in the 1968 merger of the two airlines. The aircraft was the first twin-engine passenger plane to be pressurized for cabin comfort.

(*bag*) *Jack & David Bates Collection*
The 1960s Alaska Airlines Golden Nugget Jet flight bag was larger in size and bolder in color than previous versions.

(top left & right) Hollenbeck Photo
(bottom right) Tony Nazar Collection

(*top left*) Joann Osterud, the airline's first female pilot, in the cockpit of an Alaska Airlines deHavilland DHC-6 Twin Otter.

(*top right*) On a slushy field in Wrangell, Alaska, crews load a Golden Nugget Twin Otter for a flight.

(*bottom right*) Pilots of the Golden Nugget Twin Otter visit while an Alaska Coastal Airlines delivery truck is unloaded in Wrangell.

(top left) Ron Suttell Photo
(middle) Alaska Airlines Collection
(bottom) Bodding Family Collection

(*top left*) An Alaska Airlines Golden Nugget Grumman Goose floats next to a dock along the shores of Ketchikan, in 1972.

(*middle*) Four Alaska Airlines Golden Nugget Grumman Goose line the dock in Ketchikan. These rugged amphibious aircraft were essential to the development of Southeast Alaska air service.

(*bottom*) Captain Gerald A. "Bud" Bodding after his last flight as an Alaska Airlines pilot. Called "Father Goose," he was a legend in Southeast Alaska.

(*top*) Post merger with Alaska Coastal-Ellis, passengers gather at the airport in Petersburg, Alaska, in anticipation of a flight onboard this Alaska Airlines Consolidated PBY-5A Super Catalina. The famed aircraft was used for reconnaissance and rescue in World War II. After the war, they were converted to civilian transports.

(*bottom*) An Alaska Airlines pilot stands on his Golden Nugget Grumman Goose while passengers and luggage are loaded into a company van to be driven into the town of Wrangell, Alaska.

(*top*) *Ron Suttell Collection*
(*bottom*) *Alaska Airlines Collection*

(left) On a red dirt runway near Macuma, Ecuador, an Alaska Airlines Golden Nugget Lockheed L-382 (commercial version of the military C-130) Hercules freighter is being unloaded. The airline had a contract with Texaco to haul oil rigs into remote sites in South America in the mid-1960s.

(bottom) American troops pass an Alaska Airlines Hercules on a war-torn Vietnam runway in the 1960s. Designed for the Air Force in 1952, the military versions had three-bladed props. Alaska ordered the Hercules with four blades, giving it the ability to land and take off in a shorter area.

(left) Alaska Airlines Collection
(bottom) Ron Suttell Collection

Alaska Airlines had six Lockheed L-382 "Hercules" freighters to support North Slope oil production, although only three were in service at any single time. These mighty aircraft were the only means of carrying the huge and heavy drilling rig components, equipment and supplies. The Hercules were in constant use flying to Sagwon, the original airfield in the North Slope before Prudhoe Bay was opened, and back to Fairbanks in the mid-1960s.

(*above left*) An Alaska Airlines Golden Nugget Freighter rolls off Lockheed's Marietta, Georgia, assembly line in the mid-1960s. Alaska became the first commercial airline to operate the L-382.

(*bottom*) An L-382 Hercules starts its engines in preparation for takeoff from Prudhoe Bay, Alaska, in 1969. The rugged plane was ideal for the gravel, dirt and frozen runways of Alaska. It could haul up to 50,000 pounds of cargo, cruise more than 320 mph fully loaded, fly over 2,000 statute miles without refueling and land almost anywhere.

(front) Alaska Airlines maintenance inspector Sylvester "Cy" Stampulis (left) and mechanic Lowell Ashlock work on a turboprop engine of a Lockheed L-382 Hercules in the mid-1960s.

(back) An Alaska Airlines Arctic Tours bus bound for Nome is loaded onto a Golden Nugget L-382 Hercules freighter.

GOLDEN SAMOVAR SERVICE

The Golden Samovar Era
1969 - 1973

Alaska Airlines President and CEO Charlie Willis began yet another bold move in 1969 when he introduced "Golden Samovar" service. Following three years of secret negotiations with officials of the Soviet Union, he obtained permission to take tourist charter flights into Russia during the height of the Cold War. The U.S. State Department was astonished, but didn't block the plan because it would have offended the Russians.

During the next two years, Alaska Airlines made two dozen flights to Khabarovsk, in the heart of Siberia, where the Soviet Intourist Department received the groups and conducted tours to Leningrad. Alaska leased Boeing 707s to handle the trips, which included circling the North Pole on their return.

Alaska flights throughout its system were spectacular during this era. Inflight service featured drinks poured from authentic Russian Golden Samovars, caviar snacks and vodka... accompanied by china, crystal glasses and fine silverware. Flight attendants were dressed in red and black Cossack uniforms.

It was a huge promotional success, but financially too costly to continue. In 1972, when authorization to fly permanently to Moscow and Leningrad was denied, the airline discontinued its Russian charters.

After experiencing some success in expanding Alyeska Ski Resort, the airline become even more active in the accommodations business, owning and operating several hotels and tourist lodges throughout Alaska. The airline was spending more money than it took in, however, and was headed for financial problems. Like other carriers, Alaska was hit with rising fuel and operating costs that nearly caused the airline to go bankrupt. Work on the Trans-Alaska Pipeline System was delayed, and cargo planes began to sit idle as revenues decreased. Willis brought in Fairbanks businessman Ron Cosgrave, along with his associate Bruce Kennedy, to help the airline become financially stronger. It was another bold move, although it would bring about the end of the Charlie Willis reign.

(photo) In 1969, Alaska Airlines began Golden Samovar Service to reflect its namesake state's Russian heritage and capitalize on the carrier's ground-breaking charter service to the U.S.S.R. Flight attendants dressed in Cossack outfits and used old world authentic samovars to serve Russian tea.

(pin) *Jack & David Bates Collection* This dramatic metal pin, featuring the word Alaska etched into the breast plate of the double-headed Russian Eagle, was created to secure the black sashes tied around each flight attendant's waist.

Alaska Airlines Collection

Siberia-Russia Explorers Club

ЭТИМ УДОСТОВЕРЯЕТСЯ ЧТО
(This Is to Certify That)

ЯВЛЯЕТСЯ ДЕЙСТВИТЕЛЬНЫМ ПОЖИЗНЕННЫМ ЧЛЕНОМ
(Is a Fully Accredited, Lifetime Member)

Having flown the only direct route
between the United States and Siberia;
Having duly visited within the Soviet Union's
"Great Outback" and quaffed the waters of Lake Baikal and
Having crossed the International Date Line at 53° 10'
North Latitude and 169° 50' East Longitude twice en route, on
an Alaska Airlines Jet.

ALASKA
AIRLINES

RONALD COSGRAVE
Chairman and Chief Executive Officer

(back) A Siberia-Russian Explorers Club certificate shows the route of Alaska Airlines' Russian charters, which were inaugurated in June of 1970. Newly elected Chairman Ron Cosgrave, who signed this certificate, inherited the program from the previous management, but would discontinue the charters soon after taking over as the airline CEO.

(front) This stunning Russian-styled black full-length coat and the distinctive fur hat was part of the uniform worn by Golden Samovar flight attendants.

(left) Ron Suttell Collection
(right) Alaska Airlines Collection

Introducing
GOLDEN
SAMOVAR
SERVICE

AIR TRANSPORT WORLD

A WORLD AVIATION PUBLICATION

June 1970

Alaska's Charles F. Willis, Jr.

(*left*) Alaska Airlines ran this advertisement introducing its Golden Samovar Service. Flight Attendant Dona Killeen modeled the uniform, worn by all flight attendants. Golden Samovars were used to serve Russian tea onboard flights.

(*right*) Charles F. Willis Jr., the flamboyant president and chief executive officer of Alaska Airlines, was featured on the cover of *Air Transport World* in June 1970. This photograph was taken in his office, showcasing heavy drapes, a hanging lamp and roll-top desk from his Golden Nugget Gay '90s decorations, and a Russian samovar from the Golden Samovar theme. Willis also had a fully functional beer tap in the office, which was later removed by incoming new leadership.

(back) Ron Suttell Collection
(front) Alaska Airlines Collection

RUSSIA✝SIBERIA

Alaska Airlines

(back) In June 1970, Alaska Airlines inaugurated the first charter flight from Anchorage, Alaska, to Khabarovsk, Siberia, in the Soviet Far East, with great fanfare. The flight was a public relations sensation, but the distance required Alaska to lease a Pan American Boeing 707 because the 3,800-mile trip was beyond the range of its Boeing 727s.

(front) A poster for travel agencies celebrating Alaska's flights to Siberia. The Russian flights were featured on television's "60 Minutes," in a Lowell Thomas film, and in newspapers and magazines around the world.

ALASKA ALASKA
AIRLINES

GOLDEN SAMOVAR SERVICE

SUMMER TIMETABLE

GOLDEN SAMOVAR SERVICE

(left) This 1971 Alaska summer timetable featured the airline's schedule, food, drinks and a dramatic Golden Samovar used to serve special Russian spice tea. The flight attendants also wore theatrical Russian Cossack uniforms, reminiscent of old world Czarist Russia.

(right) Alaska Airlines worked in association with the Soviet Union's Intourist Bureau to create this 1970 brochure. Moscow's St. Basil is featured on the cover.

SIBERIA
the new Gateway to
RUSSIA

ALL INCLUSIVE DELUXE ESCORTED TOURS

8 Day Siberia Exploration

1970

15 Day Comprehensive Siberia - Middle Asia - Moscow

ALASKA / Intourist
AIRLINES

The Spirit of Alaska
1973 - 1976

The 1970s saw Alaska Airlines go through a dramatic change, both in management and appearance. A new paint scheme on its fleet, was the final creative gift from Charlie Willis and Bob Giersdorf. Gone was the Golden Nugget theme, replaced by four iconic images representing the spirit and history of Alaska Airlines and its namesake state. A blue Eskimo face symbolized the strong Eskimo people; a red prospector represented the Gold Rush; a green bird totem showed off creative native traditions; and two purple orthodox church domes paid tribute to the state's Russian history.

The change in management was even more pronounced than the new color schemes. Revenues were declining due to a slowdown on the North Slope and huge increases in operational costs. The airline was struggling like never before. In 1972, the board of directors ousted Charlie Willis and named the brilliant Fairbanks

businessman he'd brought in to save the airline as CEO. With Alaska deep in debt, Ron Cosgrave set about improving profitability by reducing the workforce, dropping money-losing routes, eliminating charters and selling the Hercules fleet. He concentrated on making scheduled flights efficient and profitable. His goal was to create a professional airline built on Alaskan values of hard work and dependability.

New management brought the airline's house into order. Under Cosgrave, the company made a small profit at the end of his first year. The fortunes of Alaska Airlines were changing, and the airline was in a good position for growth with the deregulation act of 1978. When the law took effect, the carrier added more 727s and began to use the new route freedoms to serve Portland and San Francisco. It would be the first step of a steady advance into Southern California. Alaska Airlines began to prosper.

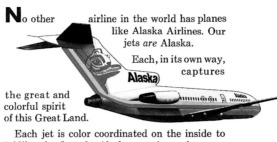

No other airline in the world has planes like Alaska Airlines. Our jets *are* Alaska.

Each, in its own way, captures the great and colorful spirit of this Great Land.

Each jet is color coordinated on the inside to fulfill and reflect the Alaska experience shown on the outside of the plane.

And each jet tells a story of Alaska that's uniquely its own.

Eskimo Alaska. The Eskimo is emblematic of a strong, tough and proud people—the original Alaskans. The color could be nothing but the cobalt blue of summer skies. Inside, the carpeting, seats and drapes are also blue, touched by the gold of summer sun that never sets.

Russian Alaska. The onion domes of old-world Russia are the classic example of early Russian influence.

The domes stand today throughout the state as evidence of the depth of our czarist past. Inside and out, the royalist purple accents this opulent era.

Gold Rush Alaska. There is no better symbol of bold, bawdy Gold Rush Alaska than the brave 1890's prospector in strike-it-rich red.

Indian Alaska. Here we demonstrate the creative traditions of the Alaskan Indian —the Alaska totem. Depicted in the rich, natural green of the verdant Southeast Alaska forest.

That's the story.

The new beautiful birds of Alaska Airlines.

But it's only a symbol of Alaska Airlines' commitment to be a better airline for Alaska.

We're going to be the best airline in the world. For Alaska. We believe it. And Alaskans wouldn't have it any other way.

Alaska Airlines

And we have more beautiful birds inside.

(top) Alaska Airlines introduced its new aircraft look and flight attendant uniforms with this "Four Culture" brochure celebrating the "Spirit of Alaska" theme. Advertising executive Bert Nordby, of Cole & Weber Seattle, created the brochure.

(bottom) The tails of the four different "Spirit of Alaska" Boeing 727s included: the 1890s Gold Rush depicted in a red portrait of a prospector; the face of an Alaska Eskimo represented the northern native cultures; a green totem face showcased the Southeast native culture; and the domes of a Russian Orthodox church displayed Alaska's Russian heritage.

Alaska

FIRST CLASS

C-12

FEDERAL REGULATIONS PERMIT
SMOKING ONLY IN DESIGNATED
AREAS ON BOARD THE AIRCRAFT

(*photo*) An Alaska Airlines Boeing 727-90C sits in the sunshine on the tarmac at Seattle-Tacoma International Airport. The purple domes of a Russian Orthodox church recall that the Territory of Alaska was owned by the Russians until 1867. The state still retains some Russian culture in many places.

(*ticket*) A first class ticket jacket from 1974 showcases the four graphic symbols of "The Spirit of Alaska" and a reminder that smoking was still allowed on aircraft.

(*letter*) A letter commemorating the opening of Ketchikan International Airport, postmarked June 30, 1973. The airport was officially dedicated on August 4, 1973, and ended the era of Grumman Goose shuttle flights between nearby Annette Island and the downtown Ketchikan Seadrome.

(*right*) Alaska Airlines Fleet Service Agent Alice Hinkle directs baggage traffic on the Anchorage International Airport ramp. She is standing near two Boeing 727-90Cs featuring the gold prospector tails in 1975.

(*below*) An Alaska Airlines Boeing 727-90C sits in the afternoon light in Nome, proudly displaying its gold prospector tail.

(*letter & below*) Ron Suttell Collection
(*right*) Hollenbeck Photo

CARRIED ON ALASKA AIRLINES FLIGHT NO. 61
720 BOEING JET, SEATTLE TO KETCHIKAN.

FIRST JET SERVICE TO KETCHIKAN INTERNATIONAL AIRPORT

Alaska Airlines

KETCHIKAN AK
JUN 30
AM
1973
99901

U S
AIR MAIL
11c

VIA AIR MAIL

DEDICATION OF KETCHIKAN'S INTERNATIONAL
AIRPORT, AUGUST 4, 1973

Alaska

N798AS

Alaska

(above) With a green Southeast totem tail, an Alaska Airlines Grumman Goose awaits passengers on the tarmac in Juneau.

(below) Alaska Airlines flew Boeing 727-100 "Combi" freighters to haul cargo and passengers throughout Alaska. Here, supplies and materials are unloaded from an Alaska charter flight onto a flatbed truck for transport to one of the many pipeline drilling camps in Prudhoe Bay, supporting exploration of oil and gas in the early 1970s.

(next page ad) Photographed for several advertising campaigns, Beverly Mahon-Becklund became a flight attendant for Alaska Airlines in June of 1972 and is still flying today.

(next page photo) Air-to-air photograph of an Alaska Airlines Boeing 727-100 showcases a serious-faced Eskimo, the forerunner of today's smiling Eskimo.

Bev would like to put you on Top of the World.

A smile still goes a long way on Alaska Airlines. All the way from Seattle to Anchorage and Fairbanks.

On Top of the World Service. With people, like Bev. Sourdough

Coffee Royale for breakfast. Top sirloin with every first class dinner. And a lot more.

Ask your travel agent to put you on Top of the World. On Alaska Airlines.

Nobody knows Alaska like Alaska knows Alaska

Timetable
Effective January 9 to April 3

Alaska
Airlines

(*above*) In 1973, Alaska Airlines purchased this Boeing 720B, which is taxiing off the runway at Seattle-Tacoma International Airport. This aircraft was eventually traded to Pan American in 1975 as part of a deal to acquire five 727-100s.

(*timetable*) An Alaska Airlines timetable from the early 1970s, featuring a dramatic Southeastern native graphic design.

(*right*) LaVonne Berrysmith became a flight attendant with Alaska Airlines in 1965 and flew for 34 years, retiring in 1999. She is modeling the new uniform of the 1970s.

146

On a sunny, snow-covered winter day in 1976, an Alaska Airlines Boeing 727-100 is loaded at a gate in Juneau, Alaska. This aircraft held 104 passengers, with 12 in first class and 92 in coach.

OUR OIL RUN
Alaska Airlines to Prudhoe Bay

(back) Hollenbeck Collection: Nancy Hollenbeck Design
(front) Jack & David Bates Collection

Announcing Alaska Airlines' Pipeline Express:

Anchorage ● Fairbanks

Dallas ● Houston

Anchorage ● Fairbanks

Dallas ● Houston

(back) President Nixon signed the Trans-Alaska Pipeline Authorization Act, on November 16, 1973. That same year Alaska Airlines won the contract put out to bid by Alyeska Pipeline Service Company to provide airlift logistical support. This poster was designed to celebrate the airline's addition of passenger service to Prudhoe Bay, which began on a daily scheduled basis in December 1981.

(front) "The Pipeline Express" was a two-carrier airlift created by an interchange agreement between Braniff International and Alaska Airlines in 1974. Braniff used its Boeing 727-200s to carry pipeline workers from Houston and Dallas to Seattle. Alaska Airlines crews flew the aircraft to northern destinations. The reverse took place with Alaska planes being boarded in Seattle by Braniff crews and flown south.

(*top left*) This 1975 system-wide route map show how extensively Alaska Airlines covered the state of Alaska, which included Wien Consolidated Airlines connecting routes.

(*top right*) Alaska Airlines featured the promotional tag line "Nobody knows Alaska like Alaska knows Alaska" in 1974, replacing Golden Nugget Service with Top of the World Service. Tags were pinned to each first class seat that read, "You're on Top of the World."

(*button*) *Jack & David Bates Collection* "Nobody knows Alaska like Alaska knows Alaska" button pins were made to promote the 1974 advertising slogan.

(*bottom*) An Alaska Airlines Boeing 727-100 flies against the sun in 1975.

(*top left*) Alaska Airlines Collection (*top right*) Jack & David Bates Collection (*bottom left*) Hollenbeck Photo

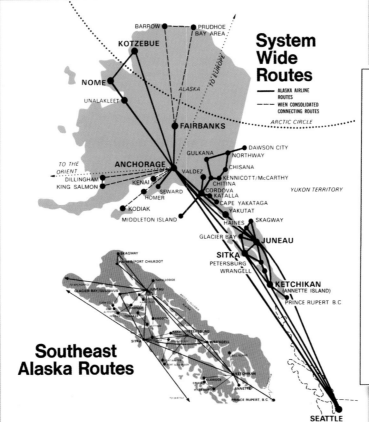

Alaska Airlines

The Smiling Eskimo
1976 - 1990

Reflecting a new attitude toward service and dependability, the Eskimo face on Alaska's aircraft tail was given a smile in 1976. The airline's marketing people announced the improvement with their "Fly with a Happy Face" promotional campaign. The friendly face and great service continue in today's airline.

CEO Ron Cosgrave's former Fairbanks business partner, Bruce Kennedy, whom he brought to the airline with him, was named president in 1978. The two men began a program of expansion and prosperity. Alaska was one of the few carriers supporting the Airline Deregulation Act, which resulted in a significant period of growth in its routes and passengers. Alaska resumed service to Nome and Kotzebue and, over the next few years, increased service in California and added stops in Idaho and Arizona.

Cosgrave resigned in 1979 after an attempt to purchase Wien Air Alaska through Alaska Airlines' real estate holding subsidiary, Alaska Northwest Properties, Inc. Leadership passed to Kennedy, who at the age of 39 would steer the airline through a remarkable period of growth. Alaska became the launch customer for the McDonnell Douglas DC-9-83 in 1983. Initially, Alaska acquired six MD-83s to replace its aging fleet of Boeing 727s. Eventually, the airline operated nearly 50 MD-80s, doubling its fleet size.

In 1985, Kennedy formed Alaska Air Group, a holding company for Alaska Airlines, when the company purchased California-based Jet America, with its trans-continental routes, eight MD-80s and 750 highly motivated employees. Alaska Air Group also expanded the airline's regional capabilities by purchasing Seattle-based Horizon Air a year later. Kennedy wanted Horizon to retain its independent spirit, so it operated as a separate company. The two airlines created a formidable partnership that successfully continues today.

To improve the seasonal imbalance of Alaskan summer routes, the airline inaugurated service to Mazatlán and Puerto Vallarta, Mexico. Kennedy was touched by Russian Eskimo families in the Soviet Union sending messages to their families in Alaska by balloons. He sparked the "Friendship Flight" in 1988, which reunited a plane full of families in Provideniya, and the experience convinced him to explore schedule flights to the region.

As Alaska Airlines grew, it was committed to quality customer service, focusing on providing better food and more leg room than other carriers. Alaska continued as a leader in technological advances, most notably being the first to adopt the Head-up Guidance System in the flight deck, which aided landing in inclement weather. It was a good era for the smiling Eskimo.

Alaska Airlines Collection: Clay Lacy Aviation Photo

The serious face of the Eskimo was replaced with a gentle smile on this Boeing 727-200, which entered service in July of 1978. The 136-seat aircraft flew between Anchorage, Fairbanks and Seattle, and inaugurated service to San Francisco on May 1, 1979.

(left) Hollenbeck Collection
(right) Alaska Airlines Collection

FLY
WITH
A HAPPY
FACE
ALASKA
AIRLINES

(left) A 1976 brochure showcased the new smiling-faced Eskimo on a Boeing 727 tail with the new slogan, "Fly with a Happy Face."

(above) Ron Cosgrave *(left)*, CEO of Alaska Airlines from 1972 to 1979, and then-President Bruce Kennedy, who become CEO in 1979, stand in front of the airline's first new 727-200 being built at Boeing's Renton plant in 1978.

(*top left*) With the "Fly with a Happy Face" campaign came new flight attendant uniforms. Beverly Mahon-Becklund was cover model for this fashion brochure.

(*bottom left*) Alaska Airlines flight attendants model the newest uniforms, designed by Ingrid Lee, a fellow flight attendant. From left: Sarah Jobs, Terry Taylor, Patty Stone and Leslie Stewart.

(*right*) This map illustrates the routes of Alaska Airlines, greatly exaggerating the role of the state of Alaska in proportion to the rest of North America.

High Fashions
Alaska Airlines changes clothes.

Our own Ingrid Lee took the caribou by the horns and created this new Alaska look. Over 20 different blue-and-tan combinations. All sensational with that Top of the World smile. Ask your travel agent to see the fashion show. On Alaska Airlines.

THE STATE OF ALASKA.

Alaska Airlines has more flights to, from and within Alaska than any airline.

As you can see by the map, we can zip you to Alaska from several cities in the Lower 48. Plus we offer quick and easy connections in Seattle from virtually every other city in the country.

But we do more than just get you there. On the way to the last frontier, we'll give you a taste of genuine Alaska hospitality. Our Gold Coast℠ service means great food and drink. Plus friendly, experienced people who can tell you all about the "insider's Alaska."

For reservations and information about our economical package tours and discount fares call us or your travel agent. Because if you're mapping out a trip to or through Alaska, you really should fly there on the airline named after it.

Alaska Airlines

Fly with a happy face.

Service to Dallas/Ft. Worth, Houston, New Orleans, Chicago and Washington D.C. via American Airlines Interchange.
Alaska Airlines also serves many communities throughout Alaska via contract carriers.

You could claim $150 of free gold.

STRIKE GOLD ON ALASKA.

Starting February 8, you can discover gold on Alaska Airlines.

Because if you fly full-fare non-stop between Seattle and Anchorage, whether it's just one leg of your journey or your final destination, we'll give you one free, Swiss-minted, solid gold, 24-karat ingot worth $75.*

If you're a full-fare roundtrip passenger, you'll receive gold on the way to your destination and again as you head home. That adds up to $150 of free gold.

And there's no limit to the number of ingots you can pocket. Keep flying and keep striking gold.

Better call your travel agent or Alaska Airlines in a hurry though. Because although our gold is virtually unlimited, our seats, unfortunately, aren't.

Alaska Airlines
Fly with a happy face.

*Offer applies to full-fare Coach (Y) or First Class (F, FN) passengers. Value of gold based on retail market value in Seattle as of January 29, 1982. Offer expires March 7, 1982.

(left) Alaska Airlines inaugurated service from Seattle to San Francisco in June 1979, giving passengers a gold ingot for flying between the two former Gold Rush cities. The gold giveaway promotion was so popular it was used at times in later years. This ad ran in 1982.

(logo) With service from Seattle to San Francisco and the gold promotion, Alaska's Marketing Department rebranded its in-flight product to "Gold Coast Service."

(top right) Ron Suttell Collection
(top right) Alaska Airlines Collection
(bottom right) Alaska Airlines Collection

(top right) "Gold Coast Service" onboard Alaska Airlines' Boeing 727s became synonymous with excellence in food and in-flight service.

(bottom right) A colorful presentation of a typical "Gold Coast Service" first class meal.

Bay Tripper.
Alaska Airlines to Oakland.

Beach Boy.
Alaska Airlines to Long Beach.

Commuter Whiz.
Alaska Airlines to San Jose.

The States Of Alaska.

Alaska

Washington

Arizona

Oregon

Idaho

California

With a name like Alaska Airlines, it probably comes as no surprise that we have more flights to, from and within the state of Alaska than anyone. But our route system extends far beyond the 49th state.

We also serve a host of cities in five other western states, including all three major airports in the San Francisco area and all five major airports in the Los Angeles area. And along the way you'll enjoy our famous Gold Coast℠ service with full hot meals or generous snacks and a crew that really tries to make every flight a pleasure. So next time you're planning a trip in the west, think of us.

And try traveling in a more relaxed state.

Alaska Airlines

(*top left*) An Alaska Boeing 727-200 taxies by the futuristic Los Angeles International Airport Theme Building, home to the Encounter Restaurant.

(*bottom left*) The flags of states served by Alaska Airlines in the mid-1980s make a colorful advertisement and West Coast regional statement.

(*billboards*) Alaska Airlines used more than a dozen popular billboards to introduce its expanding service into California cities.

The sky's Alaska | the limit. Airlines

ACKERLEY

The sky's the limit.™
Alaska Airlines

Our Goal:
"To become the best airline in the world -for Alaska."

Chairman,
Alaska Airlines

Commemorating the Inauguration of
BOEING 727-200 Service
1978

(above) Billboards promoted Alaska Airlines' advertising theme, "The Sky's the Limit."

(left) This treasured plaque, made in 1978 to commemorate the start of Boeing 727-200 service, was distributed to all stations in the Alaska route system.

Captain Chuck & Gail Spaeth Collection

(*above*) An early 1980s newspaper ad promoting the skills of Alaska Airlines pilots flying to, from and within the state of Alaska.

(*right*) *Captain Stan Baumwald Collection*
Pilot's wings combine the Golden Eagle and the Star as reminders of the airline's colorful past.

(*above*) A Boeing 737-200C is unloaded as the sun rises at noon in the winter skyline of Kotzebue, Alaska. This aircraft is a "Combi," capable of carrying cargo as well as up to 111 passengers. The outside air temperature was a crisp -35 degrees Fahrenheit in early January.

(*pin*) *Nancy Hollenbeck Design*
Created for the Alaska Airlines' 50th anniversary celebration, this pin displays the first aircraft, a McGee Airways Stinson SM-8A, and the airline's modern Boeing 727-200.

(*top*) Arctic Circle Club certificate commemorates the trip for passengers who cross the Arctic Circle on an Alaska Airlines flight. The photograph is of an Eskimo whale hunter standing on an ice floe in the Bering Sea, near Barrow, Alaska.

(*bottom*) Dog musher Ted English and his team pose beside an Alaska Airlines Boeing 737-200C on the snow-covered tarmac at Anchorage International Airport in the mid 1980s.

Arctic Circle Club

This is to certify that

_____
is a fully accredited, lifetime member,
having crossed the Arctic Circle in the State of Alaska
with Alaska Airlines

Bruce R. Kennedy
Bruce R. Kennedy
Chairman, Chief Executive Officer and President

Alaska Airlines

N744AS

(*certificate*) Ethridge Design: Hollenbeck Photo
(*photo*) Hollenbeck Photo

(*above*) Passenger check-in is busy at the Alaska Airlines counter at Seattle-Tacoma International Airport in 1988.

(*left*) Nicknamed the "Mudhens" because they could be operated on muddy, gravel runways, Alaska Airlines got the first of nine Boeing 737-200Cs in 1981. These aircraft became the workhorse of the fleet for intra-Alaska passenger and cargo flying until 2007, when the last one was retired and donated to the Alaska Aviation Museum in Anchorage.

(left) Bruce Kennedy was only 39 when he became chairman of the board of Alaska Airlines. Appointed president early in 1978, he was surprised when Ron Cosgrave replaced himself with Kennedy within a year. Under the leadership of this Eagle Scout, the airline enjoyed years of prosperity and its routes expanded into Southern California, Mexico and Russia from 1979 to 1991.

(right) Alaska Airlines pilot J.M. Antisdel conducts a "walk-around" inspection of a Boeing 737-200 on the icy ramp in Nome, Alaska, in 1988.

(top left) Alaska Airlines Collection, (bottom left) Ron Suttell Collection, (top & middle right) Hollenbeck Photos, (bttom right) Alaska Airlines Collection

(*top left*) The sun seemed to shine on McDonnell Douglas when Alaska Airlines reached an agreement to purchase six of their first MD-83 aircraft, formerly designated the DC-9-83, in 1985.

(*bottom left*) Alaska Airlines was expanding its routes in California when a marketing campaign placed sunglasses on the Eskimo as a fun promotion to emphasize the new destinations and strengthen its growing presence in the Pacific Northwest and California markets.

(*top right*) Alaska Airlines Flight Attendant Barbara Zorich greets boarding passengers in 1989.

(*middle right*) Ticket Agent Kelly Mongrain works the counter at the Seattle-Tacoma International Airport in 1989.

(*bottom right*) Seattle Mechanics Ron Owens (*left*) and Ronald Maletich signal their approval of a cool California route tail promotion, after applying the decal to the Eskimo on an MD-83.

(top) Ron Suttell Collection
(bottom) Alaska Airlines Collection

(*top*) In 1985, two MD-83 Alaska Airlines planes are in various stages of completion inside the McDonnell Douglas plant in Long Beach, California.

(*bottom*) Alaska Airlines CEO Bruce Kennedy gives the inaugural speech welcoming the first McDonnell Douglas MD-83 into the airline's fleet in early 1985, in Long Beach, California. Alaska Airlines was the launch customer for this aircraft type. Two future Alaska Airlines chairmen are seen. Far left, Ray Vecci, then-VP Planning, and at far right, then-VP Marketing John Kelly. To Kennedy's left sits Gus Robinson (with sunglasses).

163

SEAHAWKS
WEEKENDER
EXPRESS

Alaska Airlines

LEADER OF THE PAC.

Alaska Airlines flies all over the Pac-10, serving Seattle, Spokane, Portland, Phoenix and Tucson. But we don't stop there.
In the Los Angeles area, we fly to five airports (L.A. International, Burbank, Orange County, Long Beach and Ontario).
In the Bay Area, we serve San Francisco, Oakland and San Jose.

In all, Alaska Airlines flies to thirty western cities in the Northwest, California, Arizona and Alaska. With a friendly, personal style that will make you feel at home.
For reservations call your travel agent or Alaska Airlines. And fly a team with one of the best schedules in the west.

Alaska Airlines
Official Airline of the Pac-10

(*above*) Seahawk I, a Boeing 727-200, takes off from Seattle-Tacoma International Airport with Mount Rainier in the background. This aircraft became the official plane of the Seahawks at its inauguration in August of 1984. When not flying the team, fans tried to book the seats of their favorite players. Brass name-plates of players and coaches were affixed to passenger bulkheads and overhead compartments.

(*front left*) This Seahawk Express brochure announced the packaging of airfare, hotels and game ticket for residents of Alaska to see the Seahawks in Seattle. This service was the beginning of Alaska Airlines Vacations.

(*front right*) Alaska Airlines became the Official Airline of the PAC 10 in the 1980s. It was the only airline, along with sister carrier Horizon Air, flying into all 10 university locations on the West Coast.

(*left*) An Alaska Airlines flight attendant showcases the uniform, food service and friendly attitude that represented Alaska Airlines in the 1980s.

(*right*) Alaska Airlines became known for outstanding cuisine in the 1970s, which continued into the 1980s. Bruce Kennedy and the Executive Committee regularly gathered for lunch in the corporate dining room ... to eat the same lunch served on flights throughout the airline's system.

BRUCE KENNEDY
CHAIRMAN

WHO IN HIS RIGHT MIND EATS AIRLINE FOOD ON THE GROUND?

The Chairman of Alaska Airlines does. So does every other key executive in the company.

It happens during our "officers' lunch"—a twice-weekly meeting where our top managers sink their teeth into important corporate issues. Such as our meal service.

After all, we want to be certain that we're serving our passengers the kind of food that we would want to eat ourselves.

That's why you can look forward to entrees like Chicken Bordelaise and Pasta Alfredo, all prepared with fresh ingredients. And served with crisp

green salads and tasty desserts.

So next trip up or down the west coast, or to Mexico, be sure to fly Alaska Airlines.

And try the Chicken Piccata. Our Chairman highly recommends it.

165

(*all*) *Alaska Airlines Collection*

Friendship Flight #1

**Nome, Alaska
to
Provideniya, U.S.S.R.
June 13, 1988**

(*left*) A young Russian woman from Chukotka province warmly welcomes the "Friendship Flight" from Nome, Alaska, to Provideniya in the Soviet Far East on the very cold day of June 13, 1988.

(*center*) Artwork created to celebrate the Friendship Flight and its mission reuniting a group of Eskimo people separated from their families in 1948, after Stalin closed the border. When the plane landed, their Siberian families enthusiastically greeted them.

(*below*) The Friendship Flight generated a huge amount of positive media attention for Alaska Airlines, including a page one article in *The Wall Street Journal,* a spread in *National Geographic Magazine* and television coverage on the "CBS Evening News." This trip prompted Bruce Kennedy to explore ways to create regularly scheduled flights to Russia.

(*front*) The Head-Up Display (HUD) was an early example of Alaska Airlines embracing new technology. The HUD enables pilots to see important information without diverting their eyes from their flight path (this view approaching Juneau). Alaska was the first airline, in 1989, to use the Heads-Up Guidance System (HGS) to land a passenger flight in dense fog.

(*back*) As the sun sets in a pink glow, an Alaska Airlines Boeing 737-200 crosses the icy taxiway in Nome, Alaska.

(front) Alaska Airlines Collection: Captain Bill Logan Photo
(back) Hollenbeck Photo

JET AMERICA

1981 - 1987

Jet America began operating in November 1981 with former Air California vice president of marketing, Skip Kenison, serving as president, aided by a small group of California businessmen. They were undercapitalized from the beginning, but started strong. A result of a public relations blitz, nearly 4,000 people swamped Jet America's Long Beach Airport home base seeking the $99 inaugural flight fare to Chicago's O'Hare Airport. A return fare of $44.50 drew some 1,200 people in Chicago. Those cities became the airline's bread-and-butter route, and in two years Jet America had driven the powerful TWA out of that market. Although the airline remained a low-cost carrier, it increased those initial fares.

With a reputation for outstanding service as well as low fares, the airline grew rapidly and added flights to a dozen major U.S. cities, including Dallas, Detroit, Las Vegas, Minneapolis, Oakland, Portland, Seattle and Washington, D.C. In 1985,

Jet America launched another successful effort by joining Disney to promote a direct route from Dallas to Long Beach Airport for people to visit Disneyland during its 30th anniversary year. At its height, Jet America operated a fleet of ten MD-80s and two Boeing 707s. Unfortunately, high aircraft leasing fees created major financial problems.

Because of Jet America's rapid expansion, the airline was constantly underfunded. Attractive national routes, a modern fleet and loyal, motivated employees drew the interest of several major carriers. Bruce Kennedy, Alaska Airlines' president and CEO, wanted this spirited carrier to be part of his company. Through a buyout offer from Alaska Air Group, Kennedy outbid Delta Air Lines to purchase Jet America. The airline continued operating independently for about a year and then merged into the Alaska Airlines system in October 1987.

(above) A Jet America plane climbs into the sky behind the tail section of another of the airline's fleet of McDonnell Douglas MD-80s. Started in November of 1981, Jet America initially operated between Long Beach, California, and Chicago, driving the long-established and powerful TWA out of that market.

(wings) *Captain Stan Baumwald Collection*
Jet America pilot's hat wings.

(top) An early Jet America route map shows some of the destinations the airline added to its original Long Beach-to-Chicago beginning.

(bottom) Jet America was under-capitalized from the beginning, but wanted high-quality aircraft. The carrier found its solution by leasing four MD-82s from Long Beach Airport neighbor McDonnell Douglas. The company also provided training facilities that Jet America could not afford. This rare photo shows aircraft registration N482AC. Originally ordered by Air Cal, but not delivered, it was registered N780JA when Jet America began operating it.

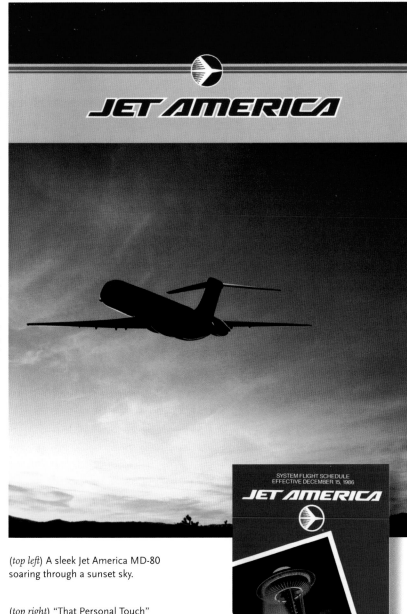

(top left & right) Alaska Airlines Collection (brochure) Gary Danielson Collection

(*top left*) A sleek Jet America MD-80 soaring through a sunset sky.

(*top right*) "That Personal Touch" tag line, used by Jet America, in an advertisement featuring Flight Attendant Kari Baca. Superior service and low fares, as well as a common fleet type and valuable slots at Orange County Airport (Santa Ana, Calif.), made Jet America an ideal carrier for Alaska Airlines.

(*brochure*) A 1986 Jet America flight schedule highlighted three of the airline's destinations: Seattle, Portland and Minneapolis.

THE AIRLINE THAT'S AT YOUR SERVICE WITH LOW FARES.

The businessmen who founded Jet America wanted to create a new approach to air travel—an airline that paid special attention to the personal needs of travelers. "That Personal Touch" at low fares has given travelers a new and better choice, with fine dining and full beverage service. An extra flight attendant for extra attention. Special touches like hot hand towels, even in coach. And with Jet America, you can fly in first class luxury at the same price as coach on many other airlines.

Today, Jet America is expanding to include more flights to more destinations. And now we offer coordinated flight connections with Alaska and Horizon Airlines for more choices than ever.

Everyone who works at Jet America takes a lot of personal pride and satisfaction in giving you the finest service, both on the ground and in the air. One flight and you'll know why they say our service has 'That Personal Touch.'

And we hope you'll take us up on it!

For reservations call your Travel Agent or Jet America.
213/595-0555   714/752-4933
800/421-7574

JET AMERICA
That Personal Touch ℠

HORIZON AIR

1981 - Present

Horizon Air was the successful idea of Seattle businessman and charismatic entrepreneur Milt Kuolt, who convinced a group of venture capitalists, notably Joe Clark and Bruce McCaw, to fund the airline. He saw the need to fill a niche market created after the Airline Deregulation Act of 1978, when larger airlines abandoned smaller routes within the Pacific Northwest. Kuolt brought together 36 enthusiastic employees and a fleet of two leased Fairchild F-27 turboprop aircraft. Horizon Air began operating in September 1981 with service between Seattle, Yakima and Pasco, Washington.

Horizon grew rapidly in the early 1980s, expanding routes and aircraft by acquiring Air Oregon and Utah-based Transwestern Airlines. Kuolt wanted passengers on Horizon to have more than just a ride — he wanted them to enjoy an excellent customer service experience, as well. Horizon soon became a public company with an initial stock offering of 750,000 shares. The stock sale was an immediate success, and the money was used to retire debt and provide funding for more aircraft and route expansion.

Horizon's proven track record attracted the attention of larger airlines. Wanting to keep its independence yet gain advantages the major carriers could offer, Horizon sold to Seattle-based Alaska Air Group, a holding company for Alaska Airlines, in 1986. The company continues to operate independently and maintains its unique character. Horizon gained the competitive advantage of connections and partnership in its sister carrier's Mileage Plan frequent flier program. Along with Alaska Airlines, Horizon code-shares with a wide range of other airline partners.

Today, Horizon is about 3,000 employees strong and serves some 40 cities in Arizona, California, Idaho, Montana, Nevada, Oregon, Washington, Alberta, British Columbia and Mexico. Horizon is recognized as one of the leading regional airlines in the country and holds the highest ranking of all regional carriers recognized by *Condé Nast Traveler Magazine*'s Readers Choice Awards.

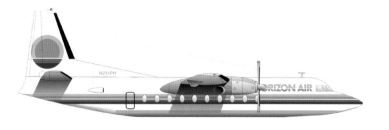

(*above*) Formed September 1, 1981, Horizon Air bought two used F-27 propjets from Quebec Air. They initially flew between Seattle and Yakima, Washington, passing by the state's towering Mount Rainier.

(*timetable*) A 1984 Horizon Air timetable featured new service from Seattle to Sun Valley, Idaho.

(*photo*) Air Oregon was founded in 1978. The carrier operated a fleet of 18-passenger twin-engine Swearingen Metroliners to several regional airports. The one shown here is on the tarmac at Seattle-Tacoma International Airport. In 1982, Horizon Air purchased Air Oregon to acquire its route system and aircraft, making Horizon the largest regional carrier in the western United States.

(*timetables*) *Mike Tobin Collection*
Air Oregon system timetables of 1980 and 1981 display their destinations.

(*wings*) *Captain Stan Baumwald Collection*
Air Oregon pilot's wings.

air Oregon
SYSTEM TIMETABLE

air Oregon
SYSTEM TIMETABLE
Service to
SIX NEW CITIES!

SAN FRANCISCO
EUREKA/ARCATA
RENO
SACRAMENTO
REDDING/RED BLUFF
BOISE

introducing the
FOKKER F27

EFFECTIVE
NOVEMBER 16, 1980

EFFECTIVE JUNE 1, 1981

N5476M

air Oregon

(*photo*) *Ron Suttell Photo*

(back) Horizon Air F-27 propjet rises toward the snow-covered mountains of Idaho in 1986.

(front) Milt Kuolt, standing next to a Horizon Air F-27, was the founder and charismatic leader of the airline from 1981 until six months after its sale to Alaska Airlines on December 31, 1986.

(brochure) A 1981 Horizon Air schedule and fares brochure includes a route map of the carrier's growing Washington and Oregon destinations.

(wings) Alaska Airlines Collection
Horizon Air pilot's wings.

HORIZON AIR
"It is our privilege to serve you"

SERVICE TO:
SEATTLE
PULLMAN
YAKIMA
PASCO
PORTLAND
EUGENE
MEDFORD

SCHEDULE AND FARES
EFFECTIVE DECEMBER 1, 1981

Welcome
Aboard

(previous page) A Horizon Air flight crew walks toward their Bombardier Q400 aircraft for a promotional advertisement. Alaska Air Group, a holding company, was formed to operate Alaska Airlines and Horizon Air under one umbrella so both could fly as independent carriers.

(above) A Horizon Air CRJ-700 climbs into a clear, blue sky on the way to one of its many regional Northwest destinations.

(magazine) Flying over Mount Rainier in Washington State is the Horizon Air 25th anniversary celebratory aircraft, a Bombardier Q-400 painted in a special scheme to capture the airline's spirited heritage. It is featured on the cover of the airline's September 2006 in-flight magazine.

Wings of the Great Northwest.

Horizon Air ®

(*above*) A Horizon Air Dornier 328-110 flies by Mount Hood in Oregon. The carrier operated these aircraft for a brief span in the early 1990s before opting to standardize its fleet to DeHavilland DHC-8s.

(*banner*) Horizon Air is one of the top regional airlines in the nation, serving the western U.S., Canada and Mexico.

(*award*) The Washington State Recycling Association honored Horizon Air with its Recycler of the Year Award in 2010. The award recognized Horizon's environmentally conscious culture.

(*photo*) A Horizon Air Q400, with the distinctive "Comfortably Greener" paint scheme, takes to the skies over Sun Valley, Idaho. The green aircraft, which symbolizes the airline's environmental efforts, uses less fuel and generates fewer carbon emissions than comparable planes.

(both) Alaska Airlines Collection

Horizon
Air

2010
Recycler of the Year

Business Generator

Washington State
Recycling Association

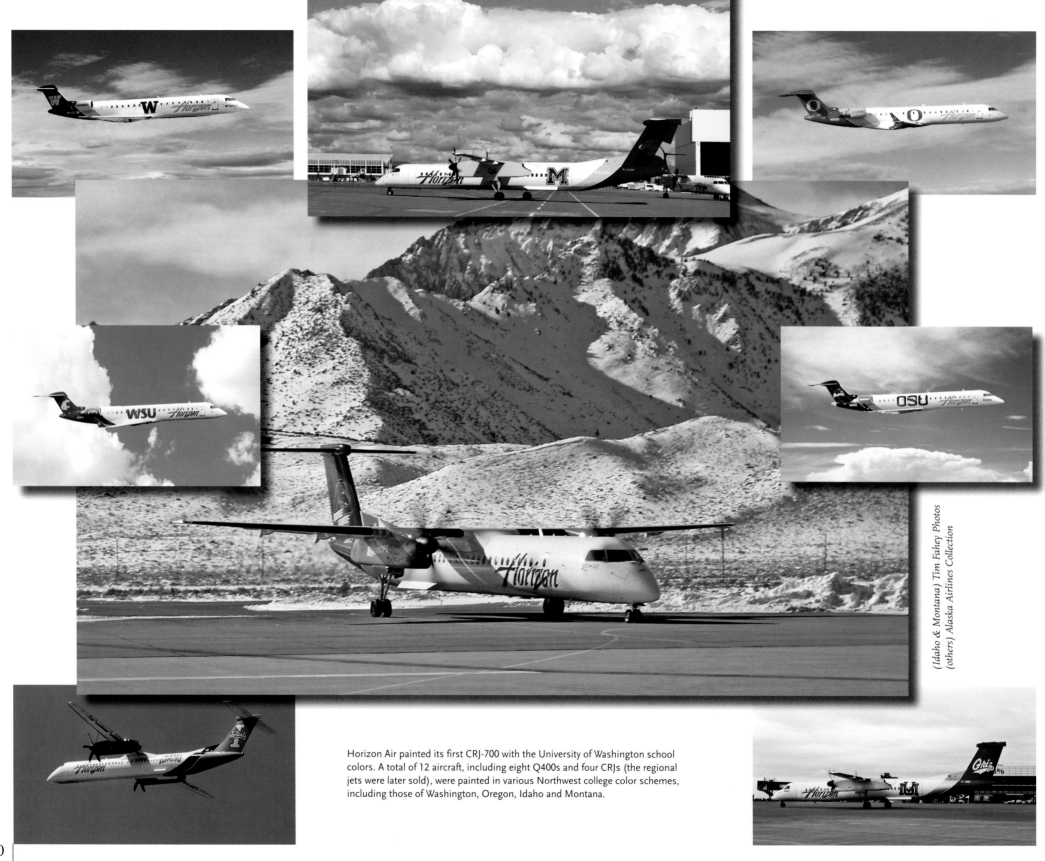

Horizon Air painted its first CRJ-700 with the University of Washington school colors. A total of 12 aircraft, including eight Q400s and four CRJs (the regional jets were later sold), were painted in various Northwest college color schemes, including those of Washington, Oregon, Idaho and Montana.

(Idaho & Montana) Tim Fahey Photos
(others) Alaska Airlines Collection

The Alaska Airlines' logo and Eskimo tail began appearing on Horizon Air planes, such as these Bombardier Q400s at Seattle-Tacoma International Airport, during the spring of 2011.

Alaska Airlines
1990 - Present

Alaska Airlines entered the modern era of aviation the same way Linious McGee started his one-plane airline in 1932, with an eye toward growth, passenger service, innovation and plenty of that adventuresome Alaskan character. The airline introduced a new, strong visual image with bold scripted lettering and more streamlined stripes. Early in this era, Alaska begin switching to an all-Boeing fleet of 737s to handle expansion across the continental United States and into Mexico.

While Alaska garnered awards for service and technological advances, profits began to diminish after nearly 20 years of solid performance. The industry endured a turbulent period in the early 1990s when fuel prices increased and fares were discounted. Bruce Kennedy retired and was succeeded by Ray Vecci, who undertook painful cost-cutting layoffs and reductions in services, eventually returning Alaska to profitability in the three years he held office.

John Kelly, a 19-year veteran of Alaska and Horizon, was named Alaska's CEO in 1995. He brought a marketing flair, can-do attitude and enthusiasm for new technology to the airline. Alaska became the first domestic carrier to offer tickets for sale online. By the middle of the 1990s, growth and profits had resumed and the airline continued to grow.

By 1997, Alaska Airlines was the tenth-largest U.S. carrier. While John Kelly remained CEO, William "Bill" Ayer became president that year. Another veteran with 15 years at Horizon and Alaska, founder of his own commuter airline and a pilot, Ayer would later replace Kelly as CEO. Along with President Brad Tilden, he

continues to lead today's modern airline through a transformation that is helping to insulate it from the industry's traditional boom-and-bust cycles.

Alaska Airlines began service to Honolulu, Hawaii, in 2007. The carrier quickly added flights to Maui, Kauai and the Big Island. Alaska also continued to be a techonology leader, equipping its fleet with a GPS satellite navigation system and the Enhanced Ground Proximity Warning System. Alaska also installed self-service kiosks that print boarding passes and it replaced ticket counters at its largest hubs with "Airport of the Future," which dramatically reduces the time customers spend checking their bags and increases productivity for lobby agents. Alaska was the first domestic airline to issue iPads to pilots, replacing 25 pounds of paper manuals and reference guides.

The airline leads the travel industry with marketing ideas, such as its association with Disney Resorts that resulted in dramatic aircraft paint schemes. The airline earned record profits for 2010 and 2011. In 2011, the airline ordered fifteen 737s, worth $1.3 billion, including the 737-900ER for high-volume and long-haul routes.

Throughout some eighty years of dynamic leadership, innovative technologies, creative marketing and turbulent times, Alaska Airlines has never forgotten its historic beginnings. The carrier's forefathers were fearless, hardworking and a little crazy — and that spirit is still part of today's airline. Alaska continues to fly the face of its namesake state in an ever-changing world, and keeps adapting to remain a vibrant airline.

This stunning air-to-air photograph of an Alaska Airlines
Boeing 737-400 was taken shortly after the aircraft was
delivered in 1993. The aircraft became the airlines' flagship,
with 40 eventually operating across its route system,
and is quiet enough to meet Stage III noise compliance
regulations in California.

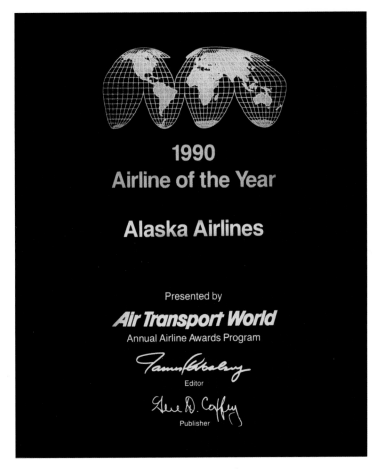

*(above left) Bruce Kennedy Family Collection
(right) Ron Suttell Collection*

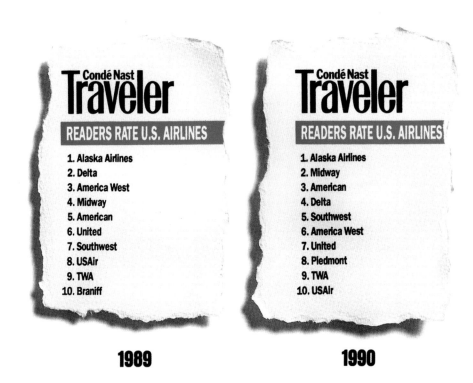

1989 **1990**

(*previous page top left*) A fresh, new graphic look came to Alaska Airlines in the 1990s. A sophisticated typestyle was created, shown here on paper products, and aircraft were remodeled inside and out. The new logo featured darker, more vivid colors and sleek parallel stripes.

(*previous page top right*) Flight Attendant Jose Carrillo, based in Portland, flashes passengers a welcoming smile.

(*previous page back*) An Alaska Airlines Boeing 737-400 soars into the setting sun, as the carrier itself seemed to soar into the rapidly changing world of air transportation.

(*above*) *Air Transport World* magazine named Alaska "Airline of the Year" in 1990 and honored the carrier with its "Airline Technology Leadership Award" in 2011. They are just two of numerous awards garnered by Alaska Airlines.

(*right*) *Condé Nast Traveler* readers rated Alaska the top U.S. airline two years in a row (eventually five years). The awards provided the perfect material for magazine and newspaper advertising campaigns.

WE'RE STARTING TO LIKE THIS MAGAZINE.

When it comes to choosing our favorite reading material, the prestigious *Condé Nast Traveler* is pretty high on our list.

Because for the second year in a row, Alaska Airlines was voted the number one airline in America by the readers of *Condé Nast Traveler*.

The results may have left our larger competitors a bit confused, wondering what sort of secret we must possess at Alaska Airlines. When actually it's really quite simple.

You see, we realize that flying probably doesn't top anyone's list of favorite things to do. So we try to make it as comfortable as possible. With good food, extra legroom and service that makes you feel like a guest, instead of a number.

Next trip up or down the west coast, call your travel agent or Alaska Airlines at 1-800-426-0333.

Because when we say we'll do everything we can to make your flight more enjoyable, you can believe it. After all, you have it in writing.

(above) These colorful tray cards are part of a series created to celebrate Alaska Airlines' expanding route system, which included the Northwest and Southwestern United States, Canada and Mexico (shown on page 188).

(below) Alaska Airlines was the official carrier of the Seattle-hosted Goodwill Games in 1990. The Goodwill Games were formed after the boycott of the Moscow Olympic games to bring American and Russian athletes together, along with other competing nations.

TEAM ALASKA

The Official Airline of the SEATTLE '90 GOODWILL GAMES Seattle Organizing Committee

(top) The McDonnell Douglas MD-80 series would fade, like this setting sun, during the first decade of the 21st century. Alaska Airlines would soon become an entirely Boeing aircraft company.

(bottom) Alaska Airlines' new visual image first appeared on the MD-80 in 1990.

(left) Alaska Airlines established regularly scheduled flights from San Francisco to the Mexican cities of Puerto Vallarta and Mazatlán in 1988 and continued to expand to additional Mexico destinations in the 1990s. This brochure advertised the airline's expansion into other popular tourist areas. By 2006, Alaska Airlines had more international flights out of Los Angeles International Airport than any other airline, due to its Mexico service.

(right) A Mexico tray card portrays the flavor and fun in the airline's service.

SYSTEM TIMETABLE

Alaska Airlines

EFFECTIVE JANUARY 12, 1992
Includes
HORIZON AIR

32785

**Seattle nonstop service to Mazatlan and Puerto Vallarta,
Mexico begins January 31.**

(above) This 1992 system timetable gave a glimpse into the beauty and vacation enjoyment in Mexico, announcing new non-stop service from Seattle to Mazatlán and Puerto Vallarta.

(right) Alaska Airlines' in-flight magazine featured a beautiful Jalisco Mexican ribbon dancer on the cover of its July 2003 issue.

Alaska Airlines

July 2003

Graceful
Guadalajara

**Alaska Airlines
introduces its newest
Mexico destination**

(brochure) In the summer of 1991, Alaska Airlines began regularly scheduled flights between Anchorage International Airport and the cities of Khabarovsk and Magadan in the Russian Far East. A Russian dancer posed for pictures after a performance in Magadan for this brochure cover.

(ad) This advertisement of Alaska Airlines' service to the Soviet Far East helped travelers visualize the destination and increased bookings. Scheduled flights into the Soviet Union was astonishing at the time and once again set Alaska Airlines apart from its competitors.

The "Best U.S. Airline" Has Touched Down In The Soviet Far East.

On June 17, 1991, Alaska Airlines became the first and only U.S. airline to fly to the Soviet Far East. That means you can now take advantage of convenient flights to the Soviet cities of Magadan and Khabarovsk while enjoying the first class comfort and service of the "Best U.S Airline," as voted by the readers of *Conde Nast Traveler* magazine each of the last two years.

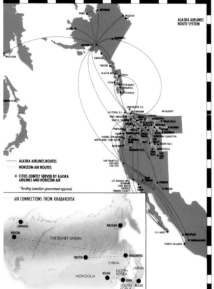

Alaska Airlines' history-making flights to the Soviet Far East depart the U.S. in Anchorage and land first in Magadan, then in Khabarovsk.

Magadan is a major port city situated on the Sea of Okhotsk. It's approximately 2,000 miles west of Anchorage.

Khabarovsk, an air, marine and surface transportation hub, is near the Chinese border in the Soviet Far East. Its location on the Amur River is approximately 3,000 miles from Anchorage. If your Far East business takes you farther than Khabarovsk, easy connections can be made to Moscow, Irkutsk and beyond.

Of course, Alaska will also make your same-day connections into Anchorage a breeze -- whether you're starting in Phoenix, Los Angeles, San Francisco, Portland, Seattle, Boise, or any other Alaska Airlines city in the West. Your travel agent or the Alaska Airlines reservation desk can give you more details and flight schedules.

View of Khabarovsk.

Join The Alaska Airlines Mileage Plan And Earn 2,000 Bonus Miles.

Be sure to call 1-800-654-5669 and sign up for our Mileage Plan Program. Identify yourself as a Soviet Far East traveler and we'll give you 2,000 bonus miles just for joining. Then every one of your roundtrip miles between Anchorage and the Soviet Far East will be credited to your new Mileage Plan account. And because our first award level is at only 15,000 miles, you'll be well on your way to a free Alaska Airlines flight with just one Soviet roundtrip.

For More Information And Our Current Flight Schedules, Or To Make Reservations, Call 1-800-426-0333.

Both First Class and Coach seating are available on all Alaska Airlines flights to the Soviet Far East. For departure times from Anchorage and arrival times in Magadan and Khabarovsk, call our toll free reservations hotline at 1-800-426-0333. Our Customer Service representatives are here to serve you 24 hours a day.

(brochure) Ethridge Design: Hollenbeck Photo (ad) Jeff Cacy Collection

HANDS ACROSS THE WATERS
©1993 MEDALLIC ART CO.-SIOUX FALLS, S.D.-BRONZE

Alaska and the Soviet Far East Together...

(medal) Bill MacKay Collection. Created by Cordova artist Joan Bugbee Jackson, this solid bronze medallion was commissioned by Alaska Airlines to commemorate its inaugural flight from Anchorage to Vladivostok in the Soviet Far East on June 8, 1993.

(poster) Renown Alaskan Artist Barbara Lavallee was commissioned by Alaska Airlines to create a triptych (set of three panels) titled "Russian-American Reunion." These paintings commemorated Alaska's new service from Anchorage to Magadan and Khabarovsk on June 17, 1991.

(photo) A Russian official scowls at the camera as arriving tourists step onto the tarmac at Provideniya in the Soviet Far East. The military operated all airports and were especially uneasy about photographs being taken.

(magazine) Ron Suttell Collection

(ticket jacket) Ron Suttell Collection: Ethridge Design

(*magazine*) John Kelly became president, chairman and CEO of Alaska Airlines in 1994, and was well into charting a new course for the airline when this 1996 *Travel Agent* cover story appeared. Kelly returned fun to the airline while keeping it economically strong. He combined low fares with customer service and a can-do attitude, adding to his drive to have Alaska Airlines continue to be a leader in customer-friendly technology.

(*award*) Alaska Airlines won this impressive "Best U.S. Airline" award as part of *Travel + Leisure Magazine*'s 1996 "World's Best Awards."

(*ticket jacket*) An Alaska Airlines Boeing 737-400 image adorns the cover of this 1997 ticket jacket.

(photo) Alaska Airlines Collection; Clay Lacy Aviation photo
(sticker) Ron Suttell Collection

OFFICIAL AIRLINE OF THE MILLENNIUM

Alaska Airlines flew into the new millennium, in this photo over Mount Rainier, as the launch customer for the Boeing 737-900 in May 2001. With an initial order of 10 aircraft, these new members of the fleet carry 172 passengers in first class and coach, and can fly farther, higher and faster than the 737-400.

Alaska Airlines created this sticker declaring itself, tongue-in-cheek, as the "Official Airline of the Millennium," when it became a launch customer for Boeing's latest aircraft

Alaska Airlines "Air Cargo" well deserves its own logo. Throughout the years, cargo revenue has been an important part of the carrier. Often, the airline was the only outside link with small Alaskan towns during the long winters. Alaska Airlines has delivered cargo around the world. Freight and mail have always been a significant part of the airline's revenue. Alaska Airlines ramp service agents push a freight pallet into position onboard a Boeing 737-200 at Seattle-Tacoma International Airport.

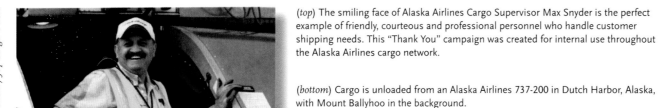

(*top*) The smiling face of Alaska Airlines Cargo Supervisor Max Snyder is the perfect example of friendly, courteous and professional personnel who handle customer shipping needs. This "Thank You" campaign was created for internal use throughout the Alaska Airlines cargo network.

(*bottom*) Cargo is unloaded from an Alaska Airlines 737-200 in Dutch Harbor, Alaska, with Mount Ballyhoo in the background.

Say Thanks.

Alaska Air Cargo is introducing a Thank-You campaign to ensure our customers know that we appreciate their business. Customers always have a choice to do business with us. In these uncertain economic times, it's even more important to thank each and every customer for shipping with us.

Let our customers know we appreciate them by saying Thank You every time you interact with them. Make eye contact. Use the customers' name. Recognize that they have a choice when they ship. And, keep providing the safe and reliable service that you do everyday. Thank YOU for taking such good care of our customers and for your support.

Alaska Air Cargo
ALASKA AIRLINES & HORIZON AIR

(left & top right) Alaska Airlines Collection: Don Conrard Photos
(bottom right) Alaska Airlines Collection: Paul McElroy Photo

(*left*) Seafood is off-loaded from an Alaska Air Cargo's Boeing 737-400C freighter. The Alaskan seafood industry and Alaska Airlines have depended on each other since the days of early bush flying. Transporting seafood to and throughout the Lower 48 states has made Alaska Airlines the largest cargo carrier (of a passenger airline) on the West Coast.

(*top right*) A freight pallet is loaded onboard an Alaska Airlines Boeing 737-200C in Alaska. This aircraft has been phased out by the newer, more fuel-efficient Boeing 737-400Cs.

(*bottom right*) Alaska Airlines has a reputation for welcoming live animal shipments, regularly hauling sled dogs and carrying all sorts of pets. A special horse stall was created for the 737-200C. This horse is comforted as Alaska Airlines personnel ready its container for loading onboard the Boeing 737-400 freighter at Seattle-Tacoma International Airport.

The lights onboard this Alaska Airlines Boeing 737-200C glow across the wet tarmac at Seattle-Tacoma International Airport. Cargo shipments are an essential part of life in remote areas of Alaska. The airline has been responsibly servicing these communities since its bush pilot days, delivering mail, supplies and contact with the outside world.

(*ad*) This Alaska Air Cargo advertisement promoted the airline's service from Alaska to the Pacific Northwest and California. Today, Alaska Air Cargo transports goods across the Lower 48 states, Alaska and Hawaii.

(*photo*) On a crisp, clear winter day in Anchorage, a pallet of cargo is about to be loaded onto an Alaska Airlines Boeing 737-400C. In 2006, the airline made a $100 million commitment to expand and modernize its cargo services.

ONLY ONE GUY FLIES MORE STUFF TO MORE PLACES ON THE WEST COAST THAN WE DO.

Ho. Ho. Ho.
You may not really believe it, but Alaska Airlines is second only to Santa when it comes to lift in the West.
We have eleven nonstops each weekday from the Lower 48 to Anchorage, with connecting and through service to Fairbanks and rural Alaska.

Five flights to Southeast Alaska.
And fifty scheduled trips between California and the Pacific Northwest.
Not only that, we can carry everything from same-day Goldstreak Express packages to seven-thousand-pound igloo containers.
Which is something nobody ever

asked for from jolly old St. Nicholas.
Give us a call with your next west coast air cargo shipment.
You just might think it's Christmas.

Alaska Airlines
AIR CARGO

Unlike Mr. Claus, our schedules may be subject to change.

(*top*) Alaska Airlines "Airport of the Future," patented in 2006, at Seattle-Tacoma International Airport eliminates traditional ticket counters with customer-friendly islands of check-in kiosks and bag-check stations.

(*middle*) First Officer Ryan Hudson checks his iPad at Seattle-Tacoma International Airport. Crucial information that pilots need is now contained on the iPad, eliminating about 25 pounds of paper traditionally carried in a flight bag.

(*logo*) *Alaska Airlines Collection*
Alaska Airlines introduced Gogo® In-flight Internet on May 19, 2010. This provides passengers with Wi-Fi service to access the Internet onboard most Alaska flights.

(*aircraft*) Alaska Airlines debuted this dot.com paint scheme on a 737-400 in 2000, showcasing its commitment to Internet technology. Pictured is the airline's latest Boeing 737-800 version of the dot.com aircraft. Alaska was the first U.S. carrier to use the Web to book travel and sell tickets on its website, www.alaskaair.com, starting in 1995. Today, the airline's online ticket sales exceed $1 billion.

(*top & middle*) *Alaska Airlines Collection: Amy McDermott Photos*
(*aircraft*) *Alaska Airlines Collection*

(top) Alaska Airlines is strongly committed to its California market, and nothing says California better than Disneyland. Alaska and Disney Resorts have created a long-term relationship that included painting four of the airline's jets with Disney characters. The result was a huge success when the Alaska Airlines Boeing 737-400 entered service early in 2003.

(bottom) It took 68 Disney artists 15 days to create the colorful "Spirit of Disneyland" scheme on the original aircraft. The amazing look, with the addition of Pluto, was recreated on this Alaska Boeing 737-900 unveiled in December 2009. The flying Disney billboards celebrate the great relationship that exists between Alaska Airlines and Disney.

Character Art provided by Disney Parks & Resorts © Disney

(*top left*) Alaska Airlines and its employees are dedicated to supporting worthy causes. The Make-A-Wish Foundation may be the most visible of these efforts, but certainly not the only organization or individuals who have been helped. The airline provides charitable contributions to all of the communities it serves. Here, 4-year-old Ramsey Farrar hugs Mickey Mouse at a Make-A-Wish event where Alaska unveiled a new Disney livery (facing page) in December 2009.

(*top right*) Disney artists created their magic on another Alaska Airlines Boeing 737-400 in 2005, the "Magic of Disneyland," featuring a flying Tinker Bell at the front and sparkling gold stars that lead to a golden Mickey Mouse ears symbol. The aircraft celebrated Disneyland's 50th anniversary on the tail and further cemented the relationship between Alaska Airlines and Disney.

(*bottom left*) The third Disney-themed jet appeared in November of 2006, with a bright blue, grinning Aladdin genie at its front. The aircraft proudly announced the commitment by Alaska Airlines and Disney to the Make-A-Wish Foundation, which supports families of children with life-threatening medical conditions.

(*top left*) Sixteen-year-old Sitka, Alaska, high school student Hannah Hamberg signs an Alaska Airlines Boeing 737-400 painted with her award-winning design. Called the "Spirit of Alaska Statehood," Hamberg's design was chosen from thousands of student submissions made from across Alaska as part of a "Paint the Plane" contest to celebrate 50 years of Alaska statehood.

(*top right*) Enthusiastic supporters of the Alaska Statehood Act rally on the tarmac beside an Alaska Airlines DC-4 in Seattle, on their way to lobby Congress in Washington, D.C. President Eisenhower signed the act making Alaska the 49th state on January 3, 1959.

(*bottom*) The colorful "Spirit of Alaska Statehood" descends toward Anchorage International Airport against the dramatic backdrop of the Chugach Mountains.

(top left) Alaska Airlines Collection: Paul McElroy Photo
(top right) Ron Suttell Collection
(bottom) Mark T. Smith Photo

Alaska Airlines unveiled one of its 737-400s painted from cockpit to tail as a gleaming king salmon in October of 2005. Funded by the Alaska Fisheries Marketing Board to promote wild Alaska seafood, the project took Seattle artist Mark Boyle and a crew of painters 24 days to complete. Known as the "Salmon-Thirty-Salmon," the aircraft is a gorgeous exhibit of art and a reminder of the strong relationship between Alaska Airlines and the Alaska fishing industry.

(*top*) Alaska Airlines' "Spirit of Seattle" Boeing 737-800 celebrates the strong partnership between the two Seattle-based companies. The aircraft is landing at Seattle's Boeing Field during early testing.

(*bottom*) The "Spirit of Seattle" sits on the Alaska Airlines hangar apron at Seattle-Tacoma International Airport beside an MD-80, marking the retirement of the older aircraft type.

(top) Alaska Airlines Collection
(bottom) Alaska Airlines Collection: Don Conrard Photo

(left) Ron Suttell Collection

(top right & bottom) Alaska Airlines Collection: Don Conrad Photos

NOSE DETAIL

8800 192015 Bright Aluminum over 8800 12384 Gray Base

8800 193009 Aztec Gold over 8800 13120 Alaska's Gold Spirit

8800 B574 Blue

8800 B70280 White
8800 B1216 Red

8800 B1216 Red- 0.5" Stripe
8800 B70280 White- 1.0" Stripe
8800 B574 Blue- 6.0" Stripe

8800 B574 Blue
6.0" Registration

8800 B574 Blue

Boeing
BOEING LOGO DETAIL

31.50"

75.50"

Starliner 75
STARLINER LOGO DETAIL

8800 B574 Blue

WINGLET INBOARD DETAIL   WINGLET OUTBOARD DETAIL

8800 B707 Gray Background
No Aluminum effect or Clear coat inboard only

BAC 70280 White
8800 B574 Blue
8800 B1216 Red

8800 192015 Bright Aluminum over 8800 12384 Gray Base outboard only Clearcoat outboard side only

See Winglet Detail

See Logo Detail

Stripes: See Tail Stripe definition for colors

8800 B70280 White 2.0" Door Bands (Typical)

Door Bands: 2.0" inner and outer 8800 12384 Gray Base

ALASKA AIRLINES

Starliner 75

N569AS

RETRO LOGO DETAIL

8800 B70280 White Star
8800 B1216 Red
8800 B70280 White
8800 B1216 Red 0.5" Stripe
8800 B574 Blue
8800 B70280 White- 1.0" Stripe
8800 B574 Blue- 6.0" Stripe
8800 192015 Bright Aluminum over 8800 12384 Gray Base

8800 12386 Lt. Gray

8800 12386 Lt. Gray

8800 12386 Lt. Gray

See Retro Logo Detail

BAC 707 Gray Wings & Struts

432.81"

ALASKA AIRLINES

ALASKA LOGO DETAIL

8800 B70280 White 2.0" Door Bands (Typical)

Door Bands: 2.0" inner and outer BAC 7099 Gray

8800 B70280 White
8800 B1216 Red
8800 B574 Blue

See Starliner Detail

8800 B574 Blue 6.0" Registration

8800 B574 Blue 31.5" Wide

8800 B574 Blue 6.0" Registration

RVSM Markings

8800 B574 Blue- 9.0" Stripe
8800 B70280 White- 1.0" Stripe
8800 B1216 Red- 0.5" Stripe

ENGINES: 8800 192015 Bright Aluminum over 8800 12384 Gray Base

8800 B574 Blue 12.0" Registration

Flag: Applied as Decal PN65-65167-13

ALASKA AIRLINES

Starliner 75

N569AS

(left) The design schematic of "Starliner 75" illustrates the special Alaska Airlines 737-800 paint scheme to celebrate the carrier's 75th anniversary. Debuted in 2007, the plane pays homage to the 1940s and 1950s style seen on the earlier DC-3s.

(top right) Stilt lady Janet Raynor, in a throwback to an earlier Gay '90s airline promotion, dances alongside "Starliner 75" at Seattle-Tacoma International Airport in 2007.

(bottom right) Alaska Airlines' 75th anniversary logo combined the Golden Eagle era artwork with the round logo and traditional North Star of the original Alaska Airlines logo, which evolved from Alaska Star Airlines.

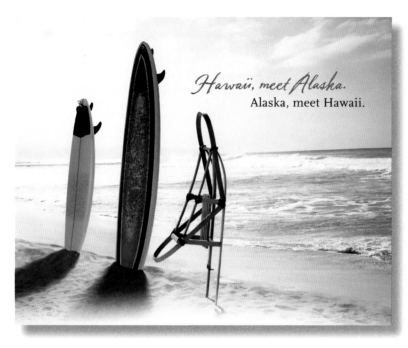

(left) An advertisement announcing Alaska Airlines' new flights to the Hawaiian Islands, begun in the fall of 2007.

(right) The October 2010 issue of *Alaska Airlines Magazine* showcases an Alaska Airlines Boeing 737-800 flying along the coastline of the Hawaiian island of Molokai. When the airline ordered 35 of Boeing's new 737-800 in 2005, their long-range capability and fuel efficiency made it possible to expand the route system. Alaska initially flew non-stops from Seattle and Anchorage to the Hawaiian islands of Oahu and Kauai.

(next page) An Alaska Airlines 737-800 flies past the stunning Diamond Head Crater, near Honolulu, Oahu, Hawaii.

(left) Alaska Airlines Collection: Design by WongDoody
(right & next page) Alaska Airlines Collection: Clay Lacy Aviation: Chad Slattery Photos

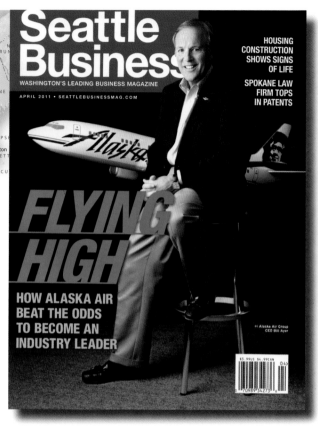

(*above*) Bill Ayer, CEO of Alaska Airlines since 2002, appears on the April 2011 cover of *Seattle Business* magazine. Promoted to the presidency in 1997, Ayer was an excellent choice. He ran his own small carrier, Air Olympia, holds a commercial pilot's license and worked for Horizon Air for 13 years before joining Alaska Airlines. His leadership has successfully steered the airline through one of the industry's most turbulent times.

(*wings*) *Alaska Airlines Collection*
Current Alaska Airlines captain's wings.

Legend

Routes served by:

— *Alaska Airlines**

······· **American**Airlines'

— ▲ **DELTA**

*Some Alaska Airlines service operated by Horizon Air or SkyWest Airlines.

HAWAI'I SERVICE

ALASKA SERVICE

MEXICO SERVICE

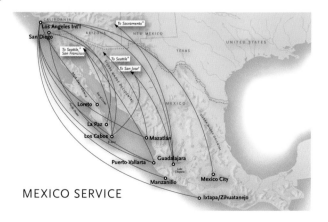

In June of 2011, Alaska Airlines was ranked "Highest in Customer Satisfaction" among traditional network carriers in North America for the fourth straight year by the prestigious J.D. Power and Associates. Alaska Airlines employees proudly display the J.D. Power Award they earned.

(*above*) Los Angeles Operations Manager Gavin Graham at Chicago's Millennium Park.

(*top right*) Anchorage-based Alaska Airlines Captain Don Burand and First Officer Amy Kohlhase on the flight deck.

(*middle right*) Cordova Ground Crew (*from the left*): Ben Johnson, Samantha Jensen, Brad Sjostedt, Lisa Jones, Jeanine Buller and John Darius.

(*bottom right*) *Alaska's World*, the airline's employee newspaper, announces the most recent J.D. Power Award on its front page.

Alaska's World

june 10, 2011

J.D. Power ranks Alaska No. 1 in satisfaction again

By Don Conrard

J.D. Power and Associates has ranked Alaska Airlines highest in airline customer satisfaction among traditional network carriers for a fourth straight year in its 2011 North America Airline Satisfaction Study. This makes Alaska the only traditional network carrier to win four J.D. Power awards.

"We're honored to receive this recognition by our customers for the fourth year in a row," President **Brad Tilden** said. "This recognition is due to the incredible efforts of our employees, who set the bar for customer service excellence."

WE'RE HONORED TO RECEIVE THIS RECOGNITION BY OUR CUSTOMERS FOR THE FOURTH YEAR IN A ROW. THIS RECOGNITION IS DUE TO THE INCREDIBLE EFFORTS OF OUR EMPLOYEES, WHO SET THE BAR FOR CUSTOMER SERVICE EXCELLENCE.

— BRAD TILDEN, PRESIDENT

(top) Tim Fahey Photo
(bottom left) Alaska Airlines Collection: Don Conrard Photo
(bottom right) Ron Suttell Collection

Follow Apolo
alaskaair.com/Apolo

Short track speed skater Apolo Anton Ohno is the most decorated American Winter Olympic champion of all time, winning eight medals. As a 2010 Olympic sponsor, Alaska Airlines encouraged people to "Follow Apolo" at the 2010 Winter Olympics by placing his likeness on a Boeing 737-800.

(left) Apolo and his father, Yuki, arrive at Seattle-Tacoma International Airport. Apolo possesses the outstanding qualities Alaska Airlines encourages: a drive to succeed, matched by dedication and hard work... all with a spirit of fun.

(*above*) In February of 2011, Alaska Airlines held a contest to design a special paint job for its sponsorship of professional MLS soccer team the Portland Timbers. Two winning designs from Paul Wright and John Bode were combined. The Boeing 737-700 "Timbers Jet" debuted at Portland International Airport on May 6, 2011.

(*left*) The March 2011 issue of *Alaska Airlines Magazine* featured Darlington Nagbe, a star player on the Portland Timbers soccer team.

(*right*) This commemorative card, with the Timbers Jet and Mount Hood backdrop, was issued to attendees at the inaugural flight ceremonies at Portland International Airport.

MLS Excitement
Portland, Seattle and Vancouver renew their soccer rivalry

Timbers Jet Roll-In

Celebrating the introduction of the Timbers Jet.

Portland International Airport
May 6, 2011

Home Grown—Home Flown
Celebrating an All-737 Fleet

Alaska Airlines Collection

(*inset*) A banner was draped on the "Spirit of Seattle," signed by Boeing workers, at the Renton plant, with messages to their friends at Alaska Airlines. The banner now hangs at the airline's hangar in Seattle.

(*back*) The "Spirit of Seattle" under assembly at the Boeing manufacturing facility in Renton, Washington. The 737-800 celebrates the partnership between Alaska Airlines and The Boeing Company.

(*next page inset*) In below-freezing weather conditions, Alaska Airlines jets leave the gate and pass between de-icing hoses. This drive-through method eliminates frost, snow and ice while reducing departure delays.

(*next page back*) During a night training exercise at Seattle-Tacoma International Airport, Alaska Airlines workers learn to operate enclosed cab de-icing equipment used for winter operations.

(*top left*) An Alaska Airlines flight attendant, in her Golden Samovar uniform, stands in the doorway of a Golden Nugget Boeing 727 in the early 1970s.

(*top right*) An Alaska Airlines flight attendant of today, Cynthia Ray, stands in the doorway of a Boeing 737.

(*bottom left*) Ticket agents and a flight attendant exemplify the friendly spirit of Alaska Airlines in the 1950s.

(*bottom right*) Today's Seattle-based Customer Service Agents (*from the left*) Santiago Santoyo, Trish James and Juan Viveros.

(top) Hollenbeck Photo
(bottom) Alaska Airlines Collection

(top) Today's mechanics (from the left): Jim Beler at fuel panel under the wing, Robert Nickles over the engine and Yuri Ivliev in the doorway work on a Boeing 737-400 in the Alaska Airlines maintenance hangar at Seattle-Tacoma International Airport.

(bottom) Mechanics work on a Douglas DC-4 in the Alaska Airlines hangar at Paine Field in Everett, Washington, in the 1950s.

(top) Cargo workers unload farm animals from an Alaska Airlines DC-3 in the 1940s.

(bottom) Nels Lawson II, with a plastic owl on his forklift (used to deter ravens and eagles while loading fish), moves cargo onto an Alaska Airlines Boeing 737-400 in Sitka, with Mount Edgecumbe behind, in 2011.

(top) Alaska Airlines Collection
(bottom) Alaska Airlines Collection: Don Conrard Photo

(top) Alaska Airlines First Officer Devon Joos checks reference material on an Apple iPad before a 2011 flight from Seattle-Tacoma International Airport.

(bottom) Captain Bill Fowler checks the instruments on a Douglas DC-4 before a flight in the 1950s.

(sticker) Alaska Airlines Collection

(top) Alaska Airlines Collection: Amy McDermott Photo
(bottom) Alaska Airlines Collection

(*above*) The modern digital cockpit of an Alaska Airlines Boeing 737-800.

(*next page*) An Alaska Airlines Boeing 737-800 flies smoothly toward the horizon, as the carrier itself confidently soars into the future. It took courage, determination, hard work, dedication, innovation and a spirit of fun to get Alaska Airlines from the Alaskan bush to today's modern age of air transportation.

Nobody knows Alaska like Alaska knows Alaska.

Alaska Airlines VACATIONS

Alaska's World

Your Flight To The Stars!
UNIVERSAL STUDIOS HOLLYWOOD

BEST U.S. AIRLINE
TRAVEL & LEISURE
1996
Alaska Airlines

Viva MexicO

I ♥

Warning:
I BRAG ABOUT ALASKA
Alaska Airlines

Alaska Airlines
CALIFORNIA DREAMIN'

BOEING 737-900
Alaska Airlines

Alaska Airlines

Fly with a happy face.
Alaska Airlines

OFFICIAL AIRLINE OF THE MILLENNIUM

Helped Make Alaska Airlines #1
Voted by the readers of Condé Nast Traveler

AMBASSADOR OF GOODWILL

SUPPORTING OUR FAMILIES & FRIENDS WHO SERVE.
Alaska Airlines

Alaska IS MY Airline

Celebrating 65 Years of
ALASKA SPIRIT

I ♥ *Alaska Airlines*

70 Years of Alaska Spirit

We're part of Disneyland!

San Francisco is an Alaska city.
Alaska Airlines

Alaska Airlines
#1
Again & Again
Again & Again

Hollenbeck Photo

THANK YOU

Hollenbeck Photo

A special thank you to members of the Alaska Airlines Book Committee, who spent countless hours cataloging photos and memorabilia, helping to ensure this book is visually and factually accurate. Pictured (left to right from the front): Paula Marchitto, Gary Peterson, Barb Norquist; (back) Tim Fahey, Ron Suttell, Mike Tobin, Rick Bendix and Paul McElroy.

One of the great joys of this project has been meeting an interesting and amazing group of people. Without the generous time and help given by the extended family and friends of Alaska Airlines, this book would still be a distant dream. This is especially true of the Alaska Airlines Book Committee, pictured on this page. A special thank you to illustrator Mike Tobin, private collectors Ron Suttell, Jeff Cacy and Don "Bucky" Dawson. Greg and Lisa Latimer brought this project and Alaska Airlines together, and we are grateful.

Hundreds of hours were spent reviewing thousands of photos, printed pieces and various memorabilia reflecting the 80+ year history of Alaska Airlines. All of those materials came from the collections of organizations and individuals. Where possible, specific credit is given adjacent to each item in the book. In addition, the authors and publishers would like to thank the following:

Alaska Aviation Museum Anchorage	Brad Burger	Bill MacKay
Alaska State Library Juneau	Eddie Coates	Captain Warren Metzger Family
The Boeing Company	Don Conrard	Tony Nazar
University of Alaska Fairbanks: Elmer E. Rasmuson Library	Gary & Margo Danielson	Lars Opland
Ketchikan Alaska Museums	Captain Charles A. Davis	Dave Palmer
Museum of Flight Seattle	Kelley Dobbs	Henry Perozzo
	Robert Ellis Family	Evelyn Jones Peters
Captain Dick Adams Family	Robert Giersdorf Family	Bryant Petitt
Jack & David Bates	Mary Goodwin	Terry Richards
Captain Stan Baumwald	Captain Charles Hall	Smoky Schnee
Joy Berger	Virgil Hanson Family	Danna Siverts
Gerald Bernhof	Carrie Jacox	Mark T. Smith
Captain Gerald "Bud" Bodding Family	Jim Johnson	Captain Chuck & Gail Spaeth
Susan Bramstedt	Bruce Kennedy Family	Captain William Stedman
D.J. Brooks	Captain William Logan	Captain Robert W. Stevens Family
	Dragon London	Barry Washington

For more information on Alaska Airlines: www.alaskaair.com.
Character & Characters, by Robert J. Serling, 2008
The Alaska Airlines Story, by Archie Satterfield, 1981

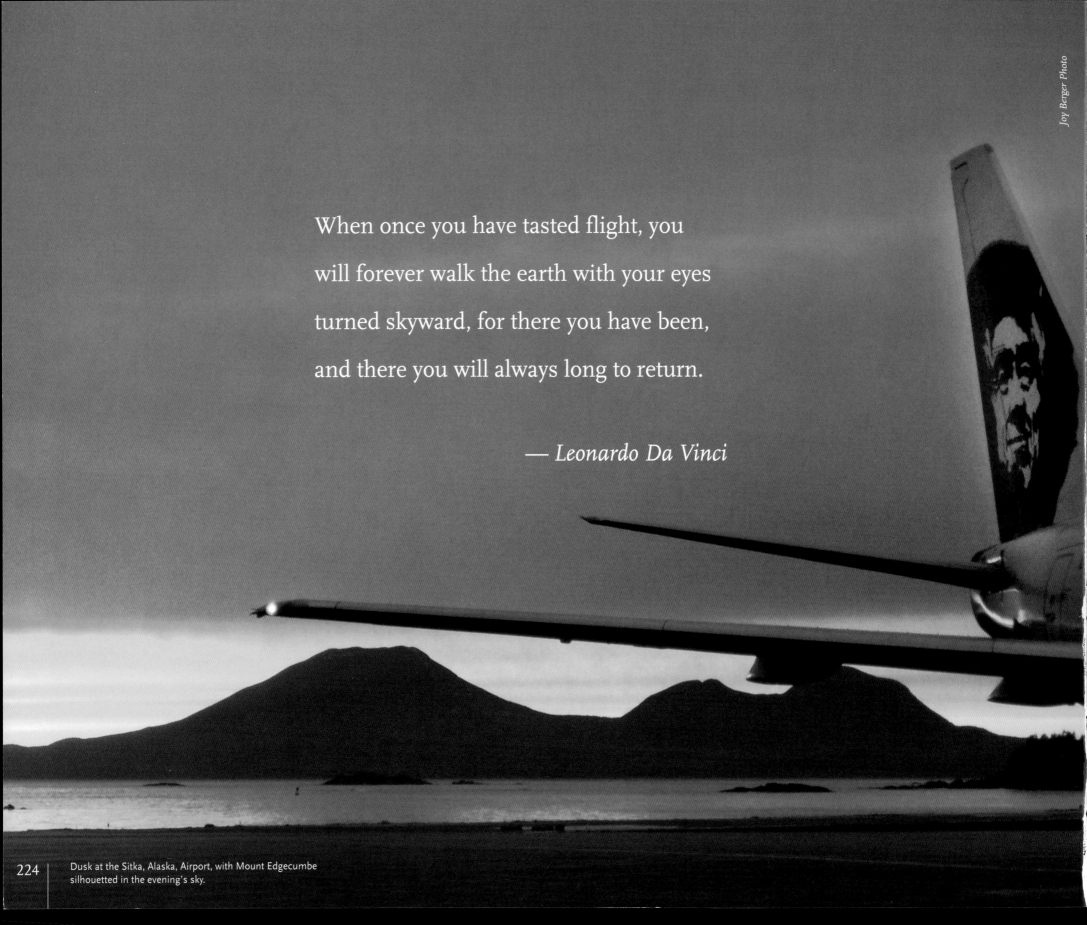

When once you have tasted flight, you

will forever walk the earth with your eyes

turned skyward, for there you have been,

and there you will always long to return.

— *Leonardo Da Vinci*

Dusk at the Sitka, Alaska, Airport, with Mount Edgecumbe
silhouetted in the evening's sky.